in Nashville, Tennessee, by Thomas Nelson. Thomas Nelson is a registered
k of Thomas Nelson, Inc.

Nelson, Inc., titles may be purchased in bulk for educational, business,
ing, or sales promotional use. For information, please e-mail
arkets@ThomasNelson.com.

Library of Congress Cataloging-in-Publication Data

Chad, 1980–
e girls who— / Chad Eastham.
.
bibliographical references and index.
978-1-4003-1300-6
woman relationships—Religious aspects—Christianity. 2. Teenage girls.
cence. I. Title.
.E26 2008
3—dc22 2008019270

Printed in the United States of America

08 09 10 11 12 RRD 5 4 3 2 1

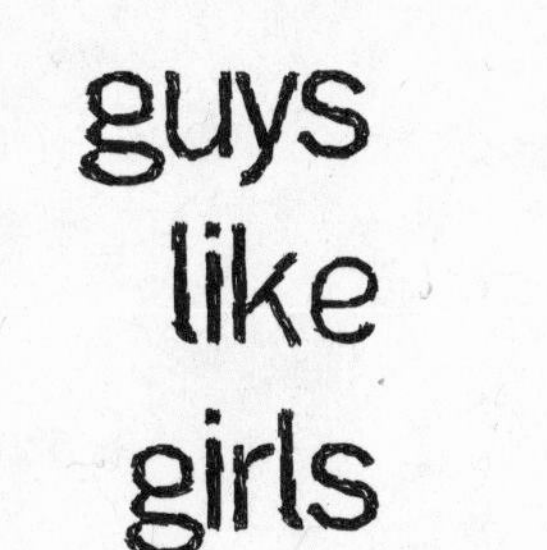

guys like girls who . . .

CHAD EASTHA

THOMAS NELSON
Since 1798

NASHVILLE DALLAS MEXICO CITY RIO DE JA

East
Gu

In
ISB
1.
3. A
BT
24

Dedication

To Laura, who is now my wife and still really likes me . . . and that makes me feel all funny inside.

Sean, you are a great friend and have helped me in my conversations, faith, work, and sarcasm . . . ever since puberty.

A special thanks to Coffee. If you were a person, I would hug you.

contents

Introduction ix

1. Are Born 1

2. Wear Jeans 11

3. Can Dance 26

4. Are Not Guys 45

5. Eat Tofu 59

6. Have Only One Face 77

7. Leave Us Alone 96

8. Have a Life 114

9. Can Spell 133

10. Can High-Five and Punch 158

11. LOL & TTYL 176

12. Can Speak Clearly 195

13. Can Read Directions 210

Acknowledgments 217

Notes 219

introduction

awkward moments

I can hear a pin drop. I'm not alone, but I can hear a whisper from a mile away. The weird thing is that I am staring at a giant arena of over ten thousand girls and they are staring back at me, and we are all completely silent. Kind of awkward, huh? Now, a group of ten girls being completely silent is highly unlikely. A room of *ten thousand* of them in total silence—unbelievable. What on this earth could have caused such rapt attention?

I have just said, "Guys like girls who . . ."

And then . . . silence.

Something has become unbelievably obvious to me every time this happens. Guys and girls have a hard time understanding each other. I am blown away by how intensely every girl is listening as they wait for me to finish the statement. In these small moments it becomes clear to me: girls want to know about guys, and guys want to look at girls. I mean . . . wait . . . know about girls.

Okay, guys like *both* of those things. The bottom line is that we all want to understand each other. There are a thousand things we do differently, from girls' natural ability to match colors and outfits to the amount of video game hours boys log, from the few emotional words guys tend to use to the abundant vocabulary girls seem to have for every thought and feeling known to man. These differences are sometimes frustrating and confusing, but mostly they are intriguing, and so we desire to know more about that person across the room.

Do you know the answer to the statement "Guys like girls who . . ."? I know the answer; do you? In fact, a lot of guys know the answer, even if they don't think they do. It is played out in their actions, their beliefs, their friendships, and their relationships. It's really important, and I promise you will be able to understand it.

I'm here to tell you what guys like in girls. It's also

important to talk about the things that they don't like. *Why?* you might ask. That's easy. We are around each other all the time; we should probably try to learn about one another. Do you wonder about guys? What they like, dislike; why they are fun, confusing, hardheaded, and softhearted? Well, if you picked up this book, of course you do. If you got it by mistake, maybe you can hurry and return it and still get a refund. But for the rest of you, the answer is a definitive yes.

So here are a few questions for you to ponder as we get started. You can write down your answers or just think about them for a moment.

- Why do certain guys go after certain girls in your class but not you?

- Why are some guys so obsessed with sex instead of actually liking girls for who they are?

- Why is it that certain girls seem to attract great guys and other girls seem to attract disrespectful guys who can act like jerks?

- Why do some girls not seem to get any attention at all from guys?

- Do you think that you attract good guys or bad guys?

- What are five things that you think guys are mostly attracted to in girls?

- Are those five things positive or negative? Healthy or unhealthy?

- Do you know the type of guys that you attract? And is this pure coincidence or do you think that it would be predictable?

If you wonder about these things, guess what? You're very normal. The teen scene can be a whirlwind. Mix that with the amount of schoolwork you have, the world of dating, your social life, sports, hobbies, your parents, siblings, three thousand texts a month, a lack of sleep, and reading this book and you can have a lot going on. Understanding the opposite sex takes a great deal of effort. But you can do it. You also have to do it. You won't always have homework, but you will always have relationships. The earlier you start understanding them, the better. It's kind of like doing your homework way ahead of time—although I never knew what that was like. Don't worry, though. Learning about one another is a whole lot more fun than studying for a geography quiz. It can even be really encouraging, as things that once seemed hazy and maybe even weird start making some sense. I hope you'll see it that way too.

"UNCERTAINTY"

My relatives tell me to act ladylike.
I can't
Swear

Punch people
Wear jeans with rips or
Get a crew cut (not like I wanted one).
I must
Wear dresses
Drink tea, with one lump of sugar
Sew
Cook
Act dainty.
Some of my friends tell me to act like a girl.
I can't
Beat up my enemies
Sit with boys at lunch (without getting teased)
Laugh at things boys think are funny.
I must
Giggle when a guy talks to me
Be boy-crazy
Talk about boys, not horses
Eat salad to maintain my slim figure (huh?).
Why can't I be
Me?[1]

—**Cathy Holland,** Williamstown, MA, grade 8

Let me start with telling you what this book is NOT. It's

not a book on "what to do to get the opposite sex to like you." It's not a text book about things guys love or hate about girls. Besides, I would never make you read a text book in your spare time. It is NOT 338 tips on how to be sexy, sassy, mysterious, taller, better than other girls, or anything dramatic of that sort. Most of those books and magazines tell you to play games to get something out of the opposite sex. Twenty tips on how to be a great flirt and 18.3 ways to make someone fall in love with your eyelashes is . . . kind of silly for real life. These things don't talk about real value. They don't help you really understand how to have great friendships. They don't help with successful dating. They don't build relationships and understanding, and they never last in the long run.

Now let me tell you what I am NOT. Even though I'm considered a teen culture expert, I don't pretend to know everything. There isn't always one answer to tough questions, just like there isn't a cookie-cutter way to have great relationships. This stuff is complicated. It's also a lot of fun. But I do spend lots of time learning, listening, and studying relationships between teens. I can tell you that I know a good deal about teens. Mostly because you talk a lot, and I like to ask questions, and being a research geek helps.

We are different, and the more we understand those differences, the happier and healthier we will be. The better relationships and friendships we will have. The more we will know what we want in our relationships and also what we don't want. We will be happier not just with the opposite sex but in every aspect of our lives.

"DO YOU THINK?"

Do you think
That being a woman
Is pretty, prim, and precise?
Showing off your body,
Flirting with the guys
Putting on mascara
So it covers your beautiful eyes
Driving around with your rich boyfriend

That's all very well
Are you trying to impress us?
Well you're not doing so well . . .[2]
—from the Lawrence School, Brookline, MA

This book is about understanding how all aspects of your life affect your relationships. It's only partly about guys; it's mostly about you. It's about understanding who you are and Whose you are. It's about understanding and honestly believing that you are of great value because God created you. He loves you, and because he loves you, you are able to love others. Plus, I think God wants us to understand and enjoy one another.

So if any of that sounds interesting or important, keep reading. I hope I can give you a small glimpse into guys' hearts and minds, with the intent to help you better understand guys and better understand yourself in relationship to guys. What do you think? Is that flashy enough for you? So here is your sneak peek into the interesting, funny, goofy, intriguing, good-smelling, bad-smelling, and uniquely different world of guys.

Chapter 1

are born

Looking for an answer to the title of this book? Then consider the following: guys like girls who . . . are born.

Yeah . . . that's it. It's actually pretty simple. You were born, weren't you? If you are reading this, then most likely you are alive; therefore at some point there's a good chance you were born. If this isn't the case, then I don't know what to say. If you were born, keep reading.

And you may not know this about yourself, but you were

born with a very specific DNA trait in your body. It's called *girl*. Congratulations on being born; you win. You were born with your girl-ness; therefore guys are going to like you. So, if I could give a simpler title to this book, it would be . . .

Guys Like Girls. The end.

Chad: Hey, Ryan, do you like girls?

Ryan: Um . . . yeah, dude, what kind of question is that?

Chad: Why do you like them?

Ryan: I don't know, man, they're girls . . . Why wouldn't I like them? They're girls. I like girls, okay?

Seriously, this is what it boils down to. Not too much more is needed in this equation. You are a girl, right? Great . . . then you have the most important part down. The hardest part is already done. Now, there may be some traits that make you more or less desirable to certain types of guys. There are behaviors and characteristics that attract certain guys and repel others. Then of course there are different stages of the whole guy/girl process depending on your age. But . . . very simply, stop and just realize that we are already made for one another. What I mean is this: God made us incomplete. Our differences complement each other.

Girls think about attraction, dating, boyfriends, and

basically all things romantic much more than guys. This may not apply to every girl, but the majority of girls think about these things from a younger age than boys. It's because your brain develops earlier than ours. Shhhhh . . . don't tell any guys I said that.

Your brains are designed so that both hemispheres work together simultaneously from an early age. I'm talking about that multitasking stuff you're really great at. Talking on the phone while doing your homework while painting your toenails while making food while laying out your outfit for the next day while thinking about the thing someone said that was really cute today. You know . . . multitasking. Even if you don't think you have this gift, the odds are you are better at it than most guys. Guys, on the other hand, think about one thing at a time. Then they think about something different.

Here's another example: guys are not always gentle. If there were only guys on earth, then there would be a lot more angry stuff going on. We would smack each other a lot more, be less sensitive, and so on. What I mean is that a girl is sometimes the natural reminder that we need to be gentle, respectful, sensitive, and caring. It's almost like a girl reminds us of the grace of God without us consciously knowing it.

God has the incredibly rough, tough, grungy, brute strength that we can recognize when boys are wrestling in the dirt. But he is also an unbelievably kind, sensitive, graceful, and calming God, which are qualities that we often think of as more feminine. I'm just generalizing here, so don't get the impression I'm saying that girls only have these traits or that guys just like to fight. I'm simply giving you a few examples of our differences here as food for thought. I'm sure girls wrestle in the dirt too . . . so if you're a girl and you like dirt, more power to you.

And no matter what you like or dislike, what your strengths or weaknesses are, whether you'd rather spend an afternoon reading a great book, hanging out with friends, or playing basketball, or all three, the most important thing is to embrace who you are and to value how God made you. Confidence and a genuine acceptance of yourself are the most attractive qualities in both guys and girls.

But not everything is simple. For example, what happens if you (a) are born and (b) like yourself, and guys still don't like you? Here's a letter from Kim:

> Hey, Chad, I'm sure you get like a million e-mails from people asking you about dating, but I have a question, well, actually a problem. . . . I do value myself. I have good morals, I like who I am, and I am not looking to date a ton of guys. I am involved

```
at my school, in sports, and I go
to youth group and I have a lot of
friends. So why don't any guys really
like me? I mean, I have a lot of guy
friends, but I want more than that.
I want guys to be interested in me
and actually be attracted to me.
Why doesn't anyone want to have a
relationship with me?
```

Pretty honest question, isn't it? And the answer to her question is that guys DO ACTUALLY LIKE HER. She probably just can't see it yet. It can be difficult if they don't like you in the way you want them to—as a girlfriend instead of as a girl friend. I'm sure it's confusing for Kim to respect herself and NOT do stupid things to attract guys (you know what I'm talking about). Maybe Kim sees one of her friends who doesn't show self-respect and a bunch of guys seem interested in her. How does that make any sense? It's the old quantity-versus-quality idea. She may not realize that even though she doesn't get as much attention as, say, someone who is really flirty, she is going to attract healthier guys later. Kim can't see the future, but her decisions are helping to shape a healthier one. Trust me—one healthy guy is better than one hundred unhealthy guys.

So, take a long-term look at guy/girl relationships. And

in the short term, give us guys a break. Life can be tough enough. We're already dealing with puberty. Do you have any idea how terrifying it is to worry about your voice cracking at any moment without warning when you are talking in front of class or to a girl you think is cute? Well, let's just say it's awful. We are trying to figure ourselves out and, believe me, that can be tough.

Guys are also on the journey to figure out qualities in girls that we respond to. So take a time-out to examine a few of your qualities with this quiz. Then, as an example, I'll give you some of what I consider my best qualities, and you can write down yours.

A Quality Quiz

1. Which of these activities best describes what you do when you hang out with friends?
   a. make sure everyone has something to eat or drink, and someone to talk to
   b. have great one-on-one conversations with a few of your friends
   c. entertain the group with your latest crazy story

2. To unwind after a hectic day of exams at school, you would choose to:

a. be active by taking a jog or exercising after being stuck in a desk all day.
b. watch the movie or TV episode you had to TiVo while you were studying.
c. be creative—write in your journal, snap some cool photos, or rearrange your bedroom.

3. If your "good skills" had to fit into one of these categories, which would it be?
a. physical (like pogo stick or bow-hunting skills)
b. intelligence (like computer-hacking skills)
c. creative (like drawing ligers and stuff)

Add up your score:

A = 3 B = 2 C = 1

Your results:

8–9

- You go out of your way for friends to let them know that you care for them.
- You "like to move it, move it" (hear King Julian in Madagascar singing) and, as a result, are fit and healthy in body and mind.
- You are a disciplined and determined person.

5–7

- You are a great listener and people love to speak to you.

» You know how to relax and, as a result, others feel comfortable around you.
» You were blessed with "brains."

3–4
» You are very social and people love to hang out with you.
» You love to express yourself creatively.
» You are inspired by the world around you.

My qualities (not all, but probably the significant ones):

- I happen to be undefeated in thumb wrestling
- I am an amazing parallel parker (thank you very much)
- I really like finding interesting ways to explain things (i.e., relationships).
- I have a knack for being an explorer. I like sleeping in the woods and other strange places.
- I go out of my way for my family and friends to let them know I care.
- I work well with other people.
- I am dependable.
- I can catch a fish with my bare hands (once anyway, but every time in my mind).

What are some of your top qualities? It's important to discover these and to feel comfortable knowing what they are. So what's great about you? Please . . . do tell.

In addition to all of those wonderful, witty things you listed, remember that you still have the number one characteristic that guys go for: you were born. So, thanks for getting up every day and being a girl. Guys appreciate that about you. Keep that in mind as you continue on. You will always have that quality that attracts guys. It's up to you to understand it and make sure it is a positive thing. Will all guys like you? I hope not. So many teens can get caught up in wanting the immediate attraction of a whole flock of boys, and, yes, I said flock. What's important isn't to attract guys but to attract good guys to your life. There is a world of difference.

Were you born? (Check one, please.)

❍ Yes

❍ No

❍ Maybe

If you checked *Yes*, please proceed to the next chapter. If you checked *No* or *Maybe*, well, that's just weird.

Chapter 2

wear jeans

Terrible Christmas Presents

I look like a baby. I am lying on the floor like a little child kicking my legs in the air like something is seriously wrong with me. And there is something terribly wrong with me, and it is on my legs. I had just gotten a really nice pair of fancy jeans for Christmas. Apparently I have a bad knack for picking jeans that are too loose on me and make me look fat.

Also, I can't believe I just said something about looking fat. Either way, I had been given a really great pair of jeans. But here I am kicking my legs in the air and I am not happy. I hate these jeans. Don't get me wrong, I'm appreciative that I got a nice present, but I don't like them. Even though they are made from great fabric and don't have any holes, I would rather burn them than wear them. And that leads me to a very important question for you.

Do you have a favorite pair of jeans? I do. I love my favorite jeans as much as I love puppies, which is a lot. They are just so comfortable. I know exactly how they feel, I know what I look like in them, and I feel more relaxed and at ease when I have them on. I make sure that I always have them with me when I go on a trip. They are kind of my go-to pants when I don't want to think about what to wear, which is 99.9 percent of the time. And of course they're great if I just need to throw something on and run out the door.

Do you have something that is your absolute favorite? Maybe it's a pillow, a sweatshirt, a hairbrush, a little brother, or some type of food? Have you ever wondered why they are your favorites? Turn to page 14 and take a second to write down a few of your favorite things and the reasons why they are your favorite things. I'll do mine first. See how this feels like teamwork without me even being there?

chad's favorite things and why:

1. My jeans: I know exactly where all the pockets are, and how much lint is in them.
2. My Quiksilver zip-up hoodie sweatshirt: It keeps me warm and makes me feel cozy but guy-ish. I throw it on after I go surfing or whenever I need to feel casual and relaxed. Sweatshirts are awesome; no explanation necessary.
3. My book bag: It has everything I need in it. My book bag can store food, books, a computer, an extra shirt, and even small dogs.

The reasons why I like my favorite things so much are these:

- They don't feel unfamiliar.
- I can take them with me to most places.
- They're just comfortable.

Now it's your turn.

Jeanships

Oddly enough, your jeans may help you to better understand relationships. In fact, relationships can be a lot like a pair of jeans. On one hand, they can be new and uncomfortable, and they don't fit right. On the other hand, we hope they will be something we really like, something we can relax in, something we know really well, and basically the most important thing . . . we hope they are really comfortable.

Some of my friends remind me of a good old pair of comfortable jeans. And the great thing about a good pair of jeans is how long they last. I had a pretty great group of friends in school. One of the best things about my friends is how relaxed we are around one another. I mean, after all, would you rather spend time around people who make you feel uptight or people who make you feel more at ease? A no-brainer, right?

Is there a point here? Yes, there is. All of the things that I LOVE are comfortable. To get your favorite jeans to the point where they are your favorite usually takes awhile. Jeans break in over time, and so do our friendships and relationships. Guys (the normal and healthy ones) understand and appreciate this. Guys like girls who are comfortable to be around and who are comfortable with who they are.

If you like guys . . . and I'm sure you do, then you need to understand this very simple secret about us: we like comfortable. So to help complete the sentence "Guys like girls who . . . ," consider that guys like things—be it jeans or girls—that are nonthreatening, relaxing, and comfortable.

Let's use, for example, Ashley and Mark. Ashley had a huuuuuge crush on Mark, who was on the varsity soccer team in their high school. He was a grade older than she was, but they had lots of mutual friends and most people at their school generally liked him. One day in the cafeteria, Ashley was paying for her lunch when someone behind her said, "Hi, Ashley!" She twirled around and saw Mark approaching with a grin on his face. They made some small talk, which eventually lead to Mark asking Ashley if she wanted to hang out at the beach with him and his friends later.

Ashley could've reacted in a number of ways, but consider these two:

1. When Ashley was getting ready to hang out, she remembered that many of the girls she'd seen Mark hanging around were preppy and pretty popular. A lot of them looked like they had come straight out of a magazine. Most of these girls only talked about things like cheerleading, fashion, and who was dating whom. Assuming that these were the types of girls Mark wanted to spend time with and was attracted to, Ashley found herself flipping through magazines looking to see how girls like that typically dress. After several long hours, her masterpiece was nothing she would normally wear, but everything she thought she should be wearing. Ashley's outfit was not the only thing that was uncomfortable. The entire time they hung out with his friends, she found herself giggling at jokes she really didn't think were funny, joining in on gossip, and faking interest in things she honestly thought were boring, like football and video games.

OR

2. When Ashley was getting ready to hang out with Mark, she remembered that many of the girls she'd seen him with were preppy and pretty popular. Even though she thought these were the types of girls Mark wanted to spend time with and was attracted to, Ashley reminded herself that he was the one who had asked her out. She decided to dress comfortably, in a way that expressed her own style. She also made it a point to be herself. They all had a blast.

While she didn't click with a few of his friends, she found that many of them sincerely enjoyed getting to know her, and respected her views and opinions, even though she wasn't football's biggest fan. And who knew that Mark loved art too? Well, Ashley did now. He didn't know much about it, but Ashley did. When he expressed his interest in art, it gave them lots to talk about. Ashley talked with him for hours about the basics of art and she had Mark's complete attention, and she even did it naturally, by relaxing and remembering to be herself.

If you're a normal person, you'd probably say the second option is the better way to go. But there are a lot of people who would actually be more likely to act like Ashley in the first scenario.

What made the biggest difference in these two scenarios? All in all, in the first scenario things were pretty awkward, and no matter how she tried, Ashley didn't think Mark was as impressed with her as she wanted him to be. If anything, Mark was more disappointed than unimpressed. Let's not forget that he invited her to hang out with him, so he was obviously interested in her. But things went awry when Ashley began trying to mold herself into what she thought he wanted rather than just being herself.

In the other scenario, Ashley's effort to be comfortable with who she was rather than who she thought others wanted her to be certainly paid off. Mark liked that she wore flip-flops, was a really good artist, and had volunteered her time at a local shelter for the past four summers. His initial interest was sparked because he could tell there was something different about her . . . she was okay with who she was.

Even if it's not a good fit relationally, healthy guys respect girls who are not afraid to be themselves.

Here, Dude . . . Take My Pants

I thought I would do a little experiment with my favorite jeans. I figured I like them so much that I would share the love. I decided to give my good friend Andrew a gift . . . my pants. So I wrapped them up and sat him down one day. With so much anticipation, I watched him open up his gift, first the bad wrapping-paper job I had done, then the used Macy's box I had placed my jeans in; finally he picked them up and stared at them.

I said, "Yea! You got my favorite jeans. Aren't they awesome? Now you can wear them."

To my surprise Andrew wasn't very happy with my gift. Maybe it was the fact that it wasn't his birthday, or that he had not asked for my jeans, or even mentioned that he liked them, but he stared at me in awkward silence for about eight seconds and then said, "Dude, seriously, you are so weird."

What? Why on God's green earth would he turn down

such an amazing gift? The reality of my little experiment was that my favorite jeans are really only MY favorite jeans, and no one else's. What would happen if you gave away a favorite item of yours to someone else, like a stranger? Odds are, even if she appreciated it, she would not appreciate it as much as you do. The reason is this: most of the time things have value because we decide that they do. It's called Rhetorical Value. Big word, but it has a simple meaning. You decided at some point in history that your favorite pair of jeans meant something special because you appreciated them and found the value in them.

There is another point about our relationships here. Does Tiffany's problem sound familiar?

> Lately I feel like I don't even know who I am anymore. My friend Shannon seemed to get along great with boys and she seemed to get lots of attention, so I started trying to do the things that she did. I thought maybe if I dressed and acted like her, they would like me as much as they seemed to adore her. I feel like I am being fake, Chad. But I don't really know how to act sometimes and I feel confused. I remember I had made

a promise with my ex-best friend Lisa that we'd never become cheerleaders, but this is my second year on the team and most of my girls are on the squad. I have found myself talking behind other peoples' backs, and I hate myself for it. And when and why did I start wearing my hair and outfits like this? Who am I? I just want to quit. I'm so confused.

—Tiffany

Have you ever seen someone like this? Or maybe you have been like this before. We try to be something we are not. Oftentimes we're not comfortable in our own skin, so we try to fit into others'. This seems to be pretty common with teens today. I can't tell you how many times some of you have shared your stories with me that sound like Tiffany's. And don't beat yourself up or feel like you are alone if you can relate to any of this. Most people can. But there is something that you must know . . .

You're Already Important

You already have been given value. I don't know if you are aware of this, or maybe you just need to be reassured.

Repeat after me: "I already have value!" I don't believe you are here on accident. I also believe that Jesus was not crazy. I believe he was telling us the truth when he said that he loves us and wants the best for our lives. I believe that God created us. This also means that he decided before we were born, the moment we were born, and every second until right now . . . that we have value.

I think we are like a favorite pair of jeans to God. These of course are my words, not his; but I still think it makes sense. And just like a favorite pair of jeans, the longer we have them, the more we love them because they make us feel comfortable and most like ourselves. I think God desperately wants us to be comfortable with ourselves and to understand that we are valued the way he values us. He wants us to fit into our own jeans. Diamonds, roses, and jeans have value because we have decided they do. God has decided that we have value. It is up to you whether or not to accept that truth.

If you have a favorite pair of jeans, you understand the joy that comes from something that feels normal, comfortable, and a part of you. I hope you can see a comparison to your own life. The more comfortable you are with yourself, the more comfortable you are with the person God has created you to be. In addition, the more comfortable you are about who you are and who you are NOT, the more you will fit into your own jeans, and the more you will start to see things, people, and relationships in a clearer and truer light.

This concept is WAY bigger than guys. It's a very simple fact: in order to be half of a comfortable relationship, we must first know and be comfortable with who we are. People go their whole lives trying to act like others—trying to change their personality traits, their looks, and their opinions—when altering those things will never help us. What will help us is to understand our God-given value and treasure the uniqueness of it.

God loves that. He loves you being you, not what's-her-name. You are not supposed to be someone else. The sooner you can start to relax in those jeans, the more you can appreciate yourself and be ready for a relationship with someone else.

do something, girl

- If you don't have a favorite pair of jeans, the perfect sweatshirt, or some other comfort item, find one. You deserve it!
- Just once when you go out with friends, don't stress over what you are going to wear. Put on those favorite jeans and a comfy shirt, and put your hair back in a ponytail. If you're really brave, forget the makeup. Guys generally like

girls who aren't overly made up. And most important, you'll feel great and you can be completely yourself.

- Call up a friend and go for a walk or exercise together. You'll have a blast talking about girl things, and your body will thank you for it.
- Try to go a week without reading a fashion or beauty magazine. Then note at the end of the week if you have a healthier self-esteem. You might be really surprised.
- Make a list of your comfort things, and when you are stressed, take some time to apply them.

Wear YOUR Jeans

Never compare your jeans to other people's. It will confuse you. If you do that, you will never see the unique person God made you to be. I always tell teens to stop looking in other people's mirrors. When you are looking in someone else's mirror, you are always looking at a slant, and you won't see the image accurately. You have a mirror right in front of you. Take some time to look at yourself through a fresh set of eyes. Perhaps you will consider looking at yourself the way God looks at you.

How Comfortable Are You?

1. If guys could rate you, what do you think your "comfort" score would be, 1 to 10?
   - **a.** 5>: guys love to chat with you
   - **b.** 5: they don't seem to mind hanging out with you
   - **c.** >5: you get the idea guys generally avoid you

2. If the doorbell rang early on a Saturday morning, your parents were working in the backyard, and you were the only one in the house, would you:
   - **a.** be too lazy to get out of bed (It's Saturday morning!)
   - **b.** throw a sweatshirt on and run to answer the door
   - **c.** take a sneak peek to make sure it's no one you know before you get the door

3. How "real" are you? What percentage of the person you portray in public is genuine and original?
   - **a.** 100 percent (You are the same person no matter where you are—at home, school, or even the mall.)
   - **b.** more than 50 percent (You may act a little different at home than you do with your friends. *Come on. Doesn't everyone?*)

c. less than 50 percent (Your parents wouldn't recognize you if they bumped into you hanging out with your friends at the movies.)

Add up your score:

A = 3 B = 2 C = 1

Your results:

8–9

» Very comfortable. You don't worry too much about what others think of you, and you stay true to what you think and feel in most situations.

5–7

» A little uncomfortable. You are a little self-conscious and make slight adjustments to your appearance and personality in an effort to make yourself and others more comfortable with you.

3–4

» Uncomfortable. You feel like you constantly have to make a great effort to fit in and make people like you. So much so, that you're not even sure who you really are anymore.

Chapter 3

can dance

I took some swing dance lessons with my friends once. I also took a dance class in school. I learned a bunch of the traditional steps and dances that people in old movies are supposed to know when they go to fancy parties. Guess what? It turns out they aren't easy, and I'm not that good at them. I end up looking kind of awkward and stiff, and I found out that my middle name is not Grace. I also learned that dancing is a lot like relationships between guys and girls.

- It usually takes a guy and a girl.
- It takes a lot of patience to learn and do the steps right.
- One person usually leads in order for it to work correctly.
- It can be difficult, but after a while things start moving in the right direction.
- You move together but also individually.
- People don't like it when you step on their toes.

Do you like to dance? Dumb question, I know; you're a girl. I ask that to groups of girls when I'm talking with them, and they always cheer and girl-scream in pure excitement of the idea. Girls tend to enjoy dancing more than guys do, from what I can see. There are even a lot of smart people out there who speculate about the biological and psychological reasons behind your desire to dance. But this isn't a biology book, so I won't bore you with that kind of talk.

However, dancing is a great way to understand relationships, so . . . let's dance. Of course, I'm not talking about that girly type of dancing that involves you in a room alone or with your friends singing into fake microphone hair brushes. I'm talking about the pretty dances, the kind that involve two people, and the ones that take considerably more effort to do correctly. I mean the waltz, the tango, and all those other exotic-sounding and complicated dances.

These might be a good place to start when it comes to the dating dance.

Yes, the dating dance, the section in your life when you not only are interested in the opposite sex but now want to get to know them, spend time talking, and go down that path of, "Hey, I think I'm interested in someone in a way that's different than I have been with other people." You know, dating!

So what in the world is dating? And how should you do it? Is there a right and wrong way? Who is supposed to ask who out? Is it okay for girls to make the first move?

Who Leads?

This is a good place to start, both in dancing and in our relationships. Consider the following questions:

Is it okay for a girl to ask a guy out? Should you ask him out or just wait for him to make the first move? Why is it a big deal if a girl asks the guy out first or makes a first move?

Do these questions sound familiar at all? They probably do. These are some of the most common questions that we get from teens about dating, relationships, and basic guy/girl interaction. And they're great questions, and there is a more creative way to look at this than a simple yes or no answer. That is what's interesting about all this stuff. There is not always a definitive answer that works for every person and every question. I know a handful of girls who asked the guy out, and things seem to work out great for them in their relationships. I also know another handful of girls who have been the leaders or the initiators, and it seemed to be more harmful than helpful. So what do we do?

The Approach—First Dance Steps

Shocking news flash: guys tend to exaggerate their confidence. No matter how confident we act, the approach—or the first steps in a dance—are really important, and they are not immediately familiar to us. Have you ever had a dance partner? Well, if you have and you are a girl, then you know that you typically don't lead in the dance. Is this sexist? No, it's not. Is it less enjoyable for you and more enjoyable for him? No, it isn't. It just means that we have different roles. Someone has to lead in the dance, and usually it is the role of the guy. I also think that there are some really important reasons why he needs to practice this role.

The Muscle

Asking a girl out involves exercising a muscle, and this is the part that isn't about you. Think about us for a moment. How would the world look if it had a bunch of men in it who didn't have any confidence? What would happen if guys never had to work for things they wanted? What would the world be like if guys didn't learn the proper steps in a dance and then they were paired up with their dance partners later? The answer is: it wouldn't look pretty. There would be a lot of self-esteem issues and a lot of people's feet would have bruises on them.

We don't just wake up one morning with confidence, the healthy kind of confidence, the kind that guys need in life. We have to build it. It's like a muscle, and it has to be exercised in order to grow. To strengthen that muscle, we have to put things on the line. We have to risk rejection in order to gain a little acceptance. We have to learn to lead. It doesn't come easily, and because of that, we tend to appreciate it more. We will tend to appreciate you more.

Not Helping

You don't really help guys when you make things EASY for them. We may feel more confident for a little while. We may even feel flattered when a girl is making the first move. But what happens when we have to step out of our comfort zone, get vulnerable, or try something new? We won't have the proper muscle. Girls tend to like a guy who is confident. Wouldn't you hate to see a guy deprived of a muscle that he is going to need in life?

Something Weird Happens

When a girl asks a guy out, something weird happens. A lot of times guys tell me that they don't tend to value something or someone that they don't have to put much effort into. For most guys, if someone gave them a car, they wouldn't value it as much as they would a car they had to work really hard to get. The same is true of girls. I think it's just how we are wired.

Take Chris, for example. Chris likes a girl named Lynn. He finally gets the nerve to ask her out to hear one of her favorite bands and have dinner. He actually decides to ask her in person instead of texting her. (Girls, take note: don't go out with a guy who asks you out by text messaging you.) He walks up to her after school, says he has a couple of tickets for the concert on Saturday, and wants to know if he can take her out to dinner and then to the concert. To his nervous surprise, she says yes.

Chris then begins to prepare. He'll have to shower. He'll need to clean his car. He'll put on nicer clothes (just a little nicer) than he would normally wear. He decides to use a little cologne (more guys should do this; some guys should wear less). He has to call and make reservations for dinner. The whole way home he is planning out in his head how he is going to make this evening really great. Why? Because he has a chance here that he doesn't want to waste. He wants to make a good impression and so he will try harder to make it because he is the one who has to put in the effort. He needs to take the lead. The odds are that the dance will go better this way.

This Is Dumb and Old-Fashioned

What about the teens who think this is stupid? Why is it a big deal if a girl asks a guy out? They would say that the point is to go out. It doesn't matter who asks whom out.

I totally get where they are coming from, but the reason it's important is . . . the future. I can't argue with a teen who has the mind-set that it doesn't matter, and I don't want to. I can just tell you this: guys tend to appreciate things they have to work for. If they don't have to work hard for something—a girl's attention, a car, or a cell phone—then they don't tend to treat it as valuable. I know this because I'm old enough to see the aftermath. It's easier to look at hundreds of teenagers, even thousands, who have told me their stories and to see how it usually ends up. The relationships aren't as healthy, and the dance seems off balance. This is not my opinion. It's just usually the way that the dance unfolds.

And more importantly, I think we can see God's design for men from the very beginning. I believe God made man to work. Adam had to work hard in the garden of Eden before God gave him Eve as a companion. God asked him to go out and name every animal. That's hard work and it takes time. It's only after this that God gives him Eve. I think if he didn't have to work so hard, he wouldn't have been able to appreciate her as much. And I often find that guys today are wired the same way.

But He Won't Ask Me Out . . .

I've heard this one a lot too. You like a guy but you don't think, or you know for a fact, that he won't ask you out. So you think the only way to get this dance started is if you are the one who initiates it. Well, part of this is true. Let me ask you another question, though. Do you really want a guy who doesn't have the courage to initiate? Do you really want someone in your life, whether a friend or a boyfriend, who doesn't want to learn how to step out of his comfort zone and do things that he needs to learn to do? I hope your answer is no. However, a lot of girls are more concerned with the here and now than they are about the future. The problem is that this may lead to developing some bad habits. I have found that girls who have healthy relationships and the ones who are sought after by guys are not just the ones who are the prettiest. They are the ones who understand the dance steps they need to take. They aren't willing to sacrifice healthy habits to get attention from a guy. They aren't as interested in having a guy like them as they are in setting up healthy parameters and spending time learning their part in this dance.

Come On, Guys

The truth is that a lot of guys face a harsh reality. In the world of casual relationships and not working hard for things we want, the outcome might be grim. These guys will have a much harder time in the future when it comes to self-sacrifice, relationships, and learning how to interact with people on a mature level. We all need to be learning our steps in the dance, and the reality is that many guys are not. I promise you it will catch up to them. The same guys who don't have to work hard for anything, risk anything, or learn to interact with girls in a healthy way, like not taking the easy way out when asking for a date, don't seem to get as much reward. They tend to have unhealthy relationships, and they end up having to learn all of this at a later time, sometimes when it seems too late.

Fairy Tales and Reality

Why is the fairy tale about the princess kissing a toad to turn it into a prince so popular? Does this sound weird to anyone else? Not just people kissing frogs, but the whole point of the story? You can't turn any guy into a prince. Guys don't become princes because of some girl. HEALTHY guys will already be princes or are well on their way to becoming one.

How about this fairy tale? You like a guy. He is perfect for you and you are perfect for him. You start dating in high school and your heart is filled with love, adoration, and affection. You hold hands, go to dances, and gaze into one another's eyes. You date for years, and when you are old enough, he buys a beautiful diamond ring, gets on one knee, and asks for your hand in marriage. He then loves you, treats you great, and tells you how beautiful you are every day for the rest of your life. Is this the picture you have in mind for your life?

The More Realistic Version

Your future probably does not include the person you are thinking of right now. *What?! How can you say that?* Well, I can say that with about 96 percent accuracy. That is the number of teen relationships that DO NOT end up in marriage.[1] It's a historical fact that most of these relationships don't last forever. I'm not trying to bum you out; I'm trying to give you something to think about. This isn't bad news. This is good news, my friend. If you know that the person you are interested in during high school probably won't be the person you marry, does that change things? For a lot of girls it does. If you knew how it was going to end, would you then start it differently? Would you open up your heart so much if you knew that you would have to do it again with someone else? Would you be physical or sleep with someone if you knew that you and he would end up with someone else?

The odds are that you wouldn't. But a lot of girls, guys too, do a funny little thing called *wishful thinking*. You want something so badly that you don't act according to reality but you act based upon what you "hope will happen." Do yourself a favor . . . stay in reality. Realize that you will probably date more than one person, and the person you really like in high school probably won't be your future husband. So with that in mind, how would things be different?

If you are dating someone and *know* that you won't marry him, what are some things that you may need to change about your relationship?

Uncomfortable Dancing

Talk about stepping on toes . . . I hope this example never sounds familiar to you:

Mark and Lindsay had been friends for a few years, and it was obvious the attraction between the two of them was beginning to grow. It was their junior year, and prom was fast approaching. Mark decided to give it a shot and ask Lindsay to be his date, which was exactly what she had been hoping for. She went to the mall with a few of her friends to get their dresses and found the perfect shoes to match. The night of the prom, Mark showed up a half hour late, *without* a corsage, to pick up Lindsay, and he didn't even apologize. To top it off, he didn't even compliment how stunning she looked; even after she asked him if she looked "okay," he simply replied with a "yes." *Well, at least he opened the car door for me*, she thought to herself. On their way to dinner, Lindsay was disappointed to learn that they were meeting up with some of his friends whom she didn't really know and who didn't even have dates. . . . She was going to be the only girl. So after a dinner of boy jokes, not being paid attention to, AND splitting the bill, they were off to prom. Upon arrival, they found out at the door that Mark hadn't paid for the tickets, and Lindsay ended up having to "lend" him the money. They found their respective groups of friends and barely saw each other from that point on. Stubborn and frustrated, Lindsay refused to ask Mark to dance, and Mark spent most of his time laughing with his friends, break-dancing, and even slow dancing with other girls! This was just too much for her, so she went to talk to Mark about it. In mid-conversation one of Mark's girl friends ran up and grabbed his hands, giggling and pulling him onto the dance floor. He showed no resistance. Lindsay was so mortified she caught a ride home with someone else and his date. Needless to say, this definitely changed her relationship with Mark.

Comfortable Dancing

What would a more comfortable dating scenario look like?

Samantha had gotten to know David pretty well over the past few months. I mean, how could she not? They basically worked together every day at the mall pretzel shop. Dave was cute. He had a great smile, loved sports, but was great at talking about other things and even listening to what Samantha had to say. The chemistry was definitely there. One day David asked Samantha if she wanted to play putt-putt that Saturday night. Her heart leaped. They had never hung out before outside of work. She went home and called several of her friends to spill the news.

Saturday night came and Samantha got a phone call from David explaining that he'd be a few minutes late. About a half hour later, her doorbell rang and it was David. After complimenting her on her hair, they walked out to his car and he opened the door for her to get in. She was unusually relaxed for being on a date and thought that it was probably because she and David had gotten to know each other prior to going on an actual date. Samantha had never played putt-putt before, but apparently she was a natural according to "coach" David! As the evening went on, it began to get a bit chilly. Without skipping a beat, David handed his sweatshirt to Samantha as they were walking to return their putters. A milkshake and several hours of laughter and great conversation later, Samantha was back at her doorstep waving to David as he pulled out of the driveway.

Ah, now that's the way I like to waltz! How about you? What is your most comfortable date scenario?

Your Dance Partner

When asking girls about their ideal dating situation, the most common word that pops out is *comfortable*. They usually prefer public places to private ones. They like it when the guy treats them with respect (ranging from compliments, door opening, and not saying anything rude or dumb), they appreciate a good conversation, and they like it when both people have a lot of similar interests. Am I close?

Comfortable dating scenarios don't necessarily mean you connect with someone romantically or even immediately. Remember, this thing is like a dance, and that means becoming comfortable with the dance, your own steps, and your dance partner. It means that you dance to get to know someone, and probably the best way to do this is when you are at ease, when you are comfortable.

Don't Dance in Gray

Sometimes when it comes to dating things can get a little gray. This means that instead of things being either black or white, with clearly defined parameters, people find themselves in some area in between where things seem fuzzy, unclear, and confusing. The dance starts to take an awkward turn. Suddenly one person is pushing, one is pulling away, you are stepping on the other person's feet, and the whole dance loses its graceful movements. When it comes to dating, this is no exception.

SHOUT OUT

A Confusing Situation?

Q: My boyfriend and I have been dating for over a year. He has a lot of friends who are girls. He goes out with girls one-on-one and says it is how he gets to "know them better." I have never felt comfortable with it, and he says he doesn't understand why. He claims he only goes out with girls who respect our relationship. But that doesn't make me feel any better. Should I move on?

A: Forget right or wrong for the moment and ask yourself this: are you becoming more confident or less confident when it comes to your friendship with your boyfriend, your perspective on guys, and the reassurance that God is at the center of your healthy relationships?

It sounds like at least one of you is not comfortable with the relationship that you have.

If you have a decent and respectful relationship, you may want to talk to him about this and tell him how you feel. If it's a miscommunication, it may be an opportunity to learn about one another. In this circumstance, if you tell him and he just doesn't care, then you need to move on. Seriously, I'm not trying to bash your boyfriend, but it's more important to take yourself out of an uncomfortable or unhealthy relationship than to try and change somebody else. It also seems like that's just a good lesson you'll need in life anyway, and this is a good chance to learn that early.

To actually answer the question, no, this doesn't really add up. What is dating? Isn't it when you go out with someone of the opposite sex to spend time together in a way that you really want to get to know them? I mean, that's simplified, but getting to know someone and doing it in a one-on-one environment is really what dating is. And, you know what, that's fine and normal . . . except if you are already in a committed relationship with someone else.

If a guy wants a girlfriend and decides to be exclusive with her, that means he doesn't take other girls out on dates. I'm a guy, and I'm pretty aware that it would have been inconsiderate and probably hurt my girlfriend's feelings if I had taken other girls out on dates. Even if I didn't call it dating, the action of what I was doing would outweigh what I told her I was doing. And you know what? Guys who do this probably know that already. The old adage here is painfully true: actions are louder than words, my friend.

So if that is indeed the case, and he won't be considerate of your relationship's status, then you really should move on and save yourself the insecurity those actions will cause in a committed relationship. But there may be something to learn there as well. Maybe you can get more into your friendships with other people. Sometimes boyfriends and girlfriends can, in fact, get in the way of us enjoying one another on just a friendship level.

Learn to dance. Have fun with it. Tread carefully. Learning your steps in this dance is invaluable. And you always have a dance partner—God. I bet he's a great dancer.

How Well Can You Dance?

1. If you feel like a wallflower at the dating "dance," do you:
   a. take the initiative to ask someone to "dance" with you?
   b. enjoy being able to build lasting friendships with other wallflowers?
   c. go home and cry yourself to sleep?

2. Now that you know a high school "dance partner" is unlikely to become a lifetime partner, will you:
   a. hope and pray that you'll be the four percent and your high school "dance" won't end?
   b. enjoy this dance, and any others that you are invited to, but not take them too seriously?
   c. stop wasting time, dump your boyfriend (if you have one), and wait 'til you leave school to dance, I mean, *date* again?

3. If you had to choose, which of these three characteristics would you rather have in a "dance partner"?

a. good looks (A good-looking partner makes *you* look good!)
b. good times (A partner who makes the dance fun is a keeper.)
c. good "moves" (A boyfriend with manners makes you feel special and impresses Mom.)

Add up your score:

A = 3 B = 2 C = 1

Your results:

8-9

» It may *look* like you are doing well at the dating dance. You're confident and proactive—but you could be setting yourself up for a fall.

5-7

» You have the right idea. You're not as flashy as some, but you're the kind of dancer a guy will want to hold on to for a lifetime!

3-4

» You are too pessimistic. There's no need to give up on dating, or to stay at it just because you think you need a partner to feel good about yourself.

Chapter 4

are not guys

I have discovered a little secret. It involves guys and body parts, but not the ones you might think. While teaching and speaking at teen health seminars, I stumbled across a funny secret. Many guys in high school think that they have a uterus.

I was hosting at a summer musical festival near Lake Winnipawhatever in Connecticut. During a break a couple of teen guys—we'll call them Joe and Chris—decided to meet up with me for lunch. They were fifteen and sixteen, had a great sense of humor, and were definitely interested in girls. I decided to do a little test on my friends. After chatting for a while, I casually asked them about what they studied in health class, and then I asked them if they knew where their uterus was located. They both sat silent for a moment, pondering, a little bit uncertain. Chris answered first. He looked at me firmly and said in a confident but slightly reluctant voice, "Um, dude . . . that is a really personal question." I held back my smile and waited to hear if Joe had an opinion on the matter. Then very curiously and slowly he lifted his finger up in a pointing motion. He started to go down his stomach, and just when I thought he was going to stop, he didn't. He kept going and going and going all the way down to his big toe. He pointed right at it, looked up at me, and waited to find out if he was right. At that moment it occurred to me that there are males operating cars on the highway who actually believe that the uterus is in the big right toe. That's just scary!

Here is the simple truth: boys and girls are incredibly different. We have lots of similarities too, but, boy, can we seem like we are worlds apart. It seems like we speak different languages sometimes. It's important for guys to try and understand girls. We have to step out of our comfort zones and put time and effort into learning about girls just like you have to do with us. Girls like guys who can understand them. Guess what? It's also true that guys like girls who can understand them. It won't happen overnight. It will take the rest of your life. Maybe a good place to start is to understand some of the fundamental differences. I hope it can give you a glance into the minds, hearts, and lives of guys in the ways that they differ from you.

Brain Food

I've said it before and I'll say it again: Waffles and Spaghetti.[1] In other words—a guy's brain and a girl's brain. If his brain is like a waffle, then hers is like spaghetti. But let's start with the basics here. Whether yours resembles breakfast food or pasta, there are two hemispheres, or sides, to your brain . . . the left and the right. The left side is the linear and logical side. It computes numbers, it uses geometry, and it logically deals with matters of the universe. The right side is the creativity center, and it is the side that emotionally connects us. Think of it this way: if the left side understands words put together to form a sentence, then the right side is what finds the meaning of those words and that sentence.

Girls, your brain could be compared to a plate of spaghetti. It's . . . mmmm . . . how do I say this . . . complicated. Put it this way. If you grabbed a noodle and followed it around a plate of spaghetti, how many other noodles would it touch? Almost all of them probably! Things are very connected in your world. How you are feeling about your body can affect your feelings about school can affect your feelings about friends can affect your feelings about what food to eat can affect which shirt you are going to wear that day . . . and the list goes on. Girls are better at multitasking than guys are. A lot of experts believe it is in your nature, and now we know that it's because both sides of your brain work together simultaneously in a way that's different from guys.

Guys' brains are like waffles. Imagine this is our brain. It has compartments and they don't all connect. Have you ever asked a guy what he was thinking and he was like, "I dunno, nothing"? He probably wasn't lying. I do it all the time, and no offense, we probably weren't thinking about you either. Here's an important thing to know about guys: we like to spend time in the compartments we are good at. Whether it's sports, flirting, math, humor, dog catching, whatever . . . we tend to look at the good aspects of ourselves and then build our self-image around those types of things. And guess what? We tend to stay away from ones we don't think we are good at, and this can last a whole lifetime. Guys tend to spend more amounts of time doing one specific thing. This isn't bad; it just means we can have different wiring. This might help you explain why it's much less comfortable for us to try and express how we are feeling about things and why it seems much easier for girls to be able to recognize their feelings and then express them.

While we all use both sides of our brain every day, guys tend to use the left side over the right side for certain things. Girls tend to use both hemispheres from a younger age, which is why you know twice as many feeling words as the average teenage male. Have you ever stopped and noticed that girls tend to say things like, "I FEEL like . . ." and guys will tend to say statements beginning with "I think that . . ."? Seriously, listen sometime for that. You'll hear it only around four thousand times a day.

These things are generalized. Guys don't only say, "I think," and sometimes they do actually express their feelings. Girls aren't just emotional beings who never think logically. There are some guys who are much more in touch with their feelings and girls who are more compartmentalized or logical in their thought process. We both use both sides of our brains, but we do have tendencies that are decidedly male or female. We have differences, and they're fun to learn about, and you're never too young to start learning.

Our Eyes Work Well

If you want to understand a basic difference between guys and girls, know this: guys' eyes work really well, usually way better than we ask them to. Guys are much, much, and two more muches, more visually stimulated than girls are. With this in mind, we often run into casual misunderstandings between guys and girls, having to do with attraction, limits, boundaries, and lots of other stuff because we fail to understand how we are different in this way.

There's a lot of evidence to back up this difference. In every text and writing from today to the beginnings of all ancient writings, we find dudes describing chicks. They mostly describe their bodies. God made woman as the manifestation of beauty here on earth. So, guess what, guys like to look at girls . . . it's not bad and it's not our fault. This is where we need each other.

Guys have a lot they are up against today. They see sexual images, pornography, soft pornography, and pictures of very lightly clothed women in almost every direction they look. Guys need to learn to show respect toward girls, and girls would do well to understand how you dress and how it affects guys.

If you think that showing your body will attract a guy to you, and THEN after he sees you he will want all the other stuff—your heart, personality, sense of humor—then you don't understand us. It doesn't usually work like that. I would tell you if it did, but it just doesn't. Teenage relationships break up, on average, four weeks or less after sexual intercourse in ninth to twelfth grade in the United States.[2] If you show a guy your body, he will want your body. You will probably draw more attention, but not all attention is good. As my friend Natalie Grant always says, "Modest is hottest." And guess what? She believes it too, and so does her husband, Bernie. You should see the way that guy stares at her . . . and it has very little to do with a sassy outfit.

Side by Side vs. Face to Face

Let's go back to the sandbox for a minute. There is an observational theory about guys and girls and their play habits. Even from a young age you can notice a difference. At the playground if there is a sandbox, or just a pile of dirt, boys will be playing there side by side. If boys are fishing, they are doing it side by side (actually, is there any other way that's not completely awkward?); if they are building a kit car, playing with G.I. Joe's, or blowing up common household objects, they are doing it side by side. It's called Parallel Play. Girls, in contrast, are much better with eye contact from a young age. When they play with their friends, they tend to sit directly across from them and have longer conversations, and the girls look at one another directly infinitely more than guys do.

Here are a few other differences that you might find interesting about us:

- When we drive, we use different sides of our brain.

Guys tend to use geometry to find direction (left side), and girls memorize landmarks to remember how to get places (right side).

- Seventy-five to ninety-three percent of interruptions in conversation are made by guys.[3]
- Within relationships, girls tend to resolve day-to-day issues, and guys usually prefer to settle huge disputes.
- Guys tend to overestimate their intelligence, and girls tend to underestimate theirs.
- Little girls in groups usually learn to blend in, be sensitive to one another's feelings, avoid boasting, and believe they're punished by exclusion when they're bossy. Generally speaking, guys think that greeting other guys in the hallway with a punch is a sign of love.
- Guys tend to do better at communication when they can focus on one thing or one topic at a time. They prefer straight-forward questions where less guessing is involved.

Vulnerable Feels Funny

There is a word that should be synonymous with teenage guys—*assimilation*. That means to blend in, associate with, not stick out from; normal things you think a normal guy is doing. This can involve dressing similar to guys in your school or group, making the same types of jokes, talking the same way about girls, to girls, around girls, and the list goes on. It means that developing guys feel most comfortable not sticking too far out from the crowd. They like to blend in, and they spend a considerable amount of time just trying to not look dumb or mess up in front of people.

Guys, teenage guys, typically say around seven to nine negative or sarcastic comments for every one positive or encouraging comment. I think that it's easier to try and be funny or sarcastic than to be more vulnerable and to talk about our feelings. Either way, guys should be nicer.

If being nice were the new cool, the world would be a different place. Unfortunately it doesn't look like that is the case. Guys are in a day-to-day struggle to find our places just like you. Guess what? Sometimes being nice, kind, and honest can make us more vulnerable. Girls tend to be more outgoing and honest with me about their insecurities, their fears, their joys, and their favorite anything. Most guys tend to be more reserved and not willing to share. A few are, but the vast majority is not. It's hard to know sometimes that guys don't have relationships, girls, friends, love, fear, and most other things figured out. It's hard because we aren't saying it, and if we did, how would people react? Bottom line: It is not easy to always be who we want to be. It is very vulnerable, and vulnerable can feel funny.

You should also know this secret: when we are alone, I

think that a lot of us guys feel like we are just big cons. We aren't as confident with ourselves as we try so hard to show the world that we are. We are afraid. Even if guys don't tend to say as much of what they are thinking or feeling as girls do, they are still thinking and experiencing a lot of the same things as girls. The more you realize how different we can be from one another, the more you realize how similar we can be too. It probably means that we are all in the same boat, and we are trying to figure out which way we need to row.

Choose a Waffle Carefully

If guys like girls who are not guys, it still leaves a lot of room for questions. So what is it that guys really want from girls anyway? That question really depends on two things:

1. The guy
2. The guy

Seriously, it really depends on who you are asking. The truth is that there are guys developing good habits at this very moment and ones developing really bad ones. Their decisions will play a big role in the things they appreciate and desire from a girl, whether it's getting coffee together or getting married. So understand and choose the waffles in your life carefully.

There are healthy guys and unhealthy guys. The way you value yourself will determine which one you attract. There are less really great and healthy guys, by the way, but quality is more important than quantity. This is very true of your relationships. If we are talking about guys who are healthy and respectful, then there is one thing their waffles will really dig about your spaghetti. It is called friendship. *Friendship is the beginning of intimacy; without it, our desire for true intimacy will not be experienced.*

If you want to understand guys, then understand friendship. This is the answer to a lot of girls' problems concerning guys. Most of what they are wondering about a guy can be figured out through this filter called friendship.

Do You Have This Filter?

- Is friendship at the root of your relationships?
- Do you want relationships that are based in the romantic before the friendship?

The truth is . . . what a guy most wants in a girl is a friend. Some people will disagree. That is because they will tend to be focused on guys who are not developing healthy habits. They might be too immature to appreciate this trait yet. Whatever the reason might be, this will still hold true: guys really like someone who is their friend. They might even be drawn to physical attraction first, but unless there is a companion, friend, buddy, and common-interests factor, it will not last. Here are some of the reasons I listed in my last book, *The Truth about Guys*,[4] why we like friends:

- Friends care enough to be honest with you.
- Friends care about you even when they know your faults.
- Friends call to see how you're doing, not just what you're doing.
- Friends know when you are hurting and will be there to listen, and they won't expect to make out after they listen.
- Friends don't look to situations to get something for themselves out of it.
- Real friends are willing to put your needs above their own wants.

If you are not a good friend, you cannot be a better anything else. You can't be a good girlfriend or a great boyfriend if you are not a friend. The root of friendship is to genuinely care about someone. Healthy guys desire this. It is not only the foundation for any kind of good relationship; it's also the most fun. If it turns out to be more than friendship, you will have a relationship that is built on something very solid to begin with. There tends to be a much more positive outcome this way. You will protect yourself, learn about the other sex, have genuine relationships, and probably laugh a lot more.

We are different. Simple enough for you? Friendship is designed to help waffles understand spaghetti and vice versa. While it's simple to say, it takes our whole life to really come to terms with this. Call it one of God's great mysteries, but it really is mysterious, isn't it? So if my young buddies with a uterus on their toe, Joe and Chris, happen to read this book, then I hope they will be reassured that they aren't alone in the world of "guys with a uterus." But they sure are, slowly, learning about the other half of the world, the one with girls in it. They are interested in the half that smells better and talks more about feelings. The first thing they will notice is that they are different. This is intriguing. This is fun. This is normal.

God made us different, guy and girl. I think he wants us to understand those differences. I think it's because the more we try to understand one another, the more we'll understand God, and the better off we will all be.

As guys will be guys, so you should be you.

How Well Do You Know Guys?

1. Which of these are true?
   a. Guys like to eat waffles
   b. Guys' brains are like waffles
   c. both of the above

2. How many things (or topics) are guys able to do (or focus on) at once?
   a. none
   b. one
   c. either of the above

3. What do healthy and respectful guys want most in a relationship?
   a. physical attraction
   b. common interests
   c. friendship

Answers:

1 = c   2 = c   3 = c

Chapter 5
eat tofu

"Tread carefully here, Chad . . ." **—Chad**

Oh no, you didn't?! Did you write about girls and their physical health and appearance? Yes, yes, I did and I'll tell you one reason, actually a couple of reasons, why. Plastic surgery for teenagers is rising exponentially each year and yet the healthy emotional state of teens is not. Seventy-five percent of female teens said that they would drastically change at least one part of their body.[1] I am confident that the number of discontented females has been going up, and their joy is going down. I could give you another thousand facts that might disturb you . . . but instead I'd like to ask you a question.

Do you know what *healthy* means?

We can look to the Bible for a great explanation: "Or didn't you realize that your body is a sacred place, the place of the Holy Spirit? Don't you see that you can't live however you please, squandering what God paid such a high price for? The physical part of you is not some piece of property belonging to the spiritual part of you. God owns the whole works. So let people see God in and through your body" (1 Cor. 6:17–20).

Are you afraid I'm going to tell you that girls need to exercise or lose weight? No thanks, I don't really feel like getting beat up today. I wouldn't dare write a chapter about that. And don't worry, you don't have to like or eat tofu either. I only eat it when I get dared, and honestly, it's usually not worth it. But even though I think that tofu tastes like toes, I do know that it's healthy.

It's no doubt that guys like girls who are healthy—not just physically healthy, but mentally, spiritually, and socially as well. But more important than getting healthy for guys is getting healthy for you. You'll feel better, look better, and become more confident.

The first step to being a healthy person is to start thinking about what health means . . .

- What does healthy mean to you?

- How and why do you think God wants us to be healthy?

- What are some things that are healthy about you?

- What are some things in your life you know are unhealthy?

Looking Good Is Not What Healthy Means

A huge part of overall health is having a healthy self-image—how you view yourself. I just read that teens will spend almost 280 billion dollars this year on . . . stuff.[2] Much of this . . . stuff . . . comes from you being confused about your self-image. In fact, most of these images are made up, pushed on you, impossible to attain, and designed to make you feel bad about yourself so you'll buy things to make you feel better again. These things you buy, of course, do not.

It's amazing what people will do to their bodies to make themselves "pretty." Stretch their lips in Africa, widen their eyes via plastic surgery in Korea, dye their skin lighter in India. The United States isn't the only country that experiences social pressures to look certain ways and has people who do extreme things to fill these "ideals."

Is it a good idea to do stuff *in order* to get people, specifically guys, to like you? In my personal and professional opinion, NO! While it's completely natural to want people to like you, it's very important how you go about it. It's a bad idea to start rearranging yourself so that you'll be liked by others. I think it's kind of the opposite. It is usually better if others like you because of who you already are.

Start looking at the healthy things about yourself. You're off to a good start with the short list above, but grab a notepad and keep a running list. Make a list of big things, little things, goofy things, odd things, and things you might not be thinking about day to day. Write them down when you think of them, and go back and review them every once in a while. It's a great way to remember the positive, healthy points about yourself. Plus, you'll be able to look back and see what a healthy person you've become!

You are just starting to develop, and there is so much more room for you to grow and find out new things about yourself. Try and focus on your positive qualities. Embrace these things. I find that some of my goofiest qualities are things that people like about me. When you start to focus on the positive things more and the negative things less, something strange will start to happen. You will start to view yourself in a healthier way.

Your Beauty

Truth about guys: the majority of guys desire to be physically attracted to a girl, but this does NOT mean you need to look like anyone on TV or in magazines or whatever. Just because you might hear some guys talking about how "hot" some girl is doesn't mean you have to feel like you should look like or be like her. Happiness is way better than hotness. Happiness is contagious. Hotness is contagious, but it's more like the flu contagious. Happiness and joy are beauty, and they start on the inside. Also, they don't require fancy pants.

Your beauty means way more than your face. Unfortunately most of the advertisements stop there, unless they move on to some other feature strictly about your body. Just because you see it in magazines does not mean it's true. Beauty encompasses a lot of things. Let's start with something we can't always see with our eyes, but we sense it instead.

Your Spirit

Your relationship with God supersedes all other types of beauty. Nurturing that relationship is kind of like a daily moisturizer for your heart and soul. It affects all the other parts of you. You can be the prettiest person on the planet, but you will never be as beautiful as you could be until you let God fill you up with his truth and love.

You can have a great image of yourself because God has one of you. That means you just have to discover it. His opinion matters more than all guys' opinions put together, and the great news is, if you have faith in this, then you're already putting effort into someone and something that matters. That is a great start to having a positive self-image.

Your Lifestyle

Your lifestyle encompasses all the things you do with your friends and your family, and what you're into. This has a lot to do with your health. Some people's lifestyles are really easy and well balanced. Others are pretty lopsided and unbalanced. Do you find that you spend all of your time with just your friends, or just your boyfriend, or maybe it is academics, perhaps volleyball? Either way it's going to be important to strike a balance with all of these things, and that is true not just in high school. Remember that a lot of patterns we set in our teenage years can stick with us for a long time.

Where Do You Spend Your Time?

1. Where is your mind most of the day?
   a. on the day's activities
   b. dreaming about your boyfriend or the guy you like
   c. working out how to improve your physical appearance

2. How often do you hang out with God?
   a. every day for a bit
   b. if you're feeling low
   c. when you have time or think of him

3. If, on a Saturday afternoon, your dad excitedly told you he bought tickets for the entire family to see a play that night, but your boyfriend wanted to treat you to dinner and a movie the same night, and the truth was you really needed to spend the night studying for a test on Monday, what would you do?
   a. join your family for the play and study a little later than usual
   b. tell your dad your boyfriend had already invited you out and that it wouldn't be right to cancel now
   c. stay at home and study

Add up your score:
A = 3 B = 2 C = 1

Your results:

8–9

» You seem to spend your time wisely—it appears God, family, and a balance of your own activities are important to you.

5–7

» Warning! You may be a clingbot. Your time may be centered too much on guys. Do you need attention from a guy to feel good about yourself?

3–4

» You could be a little self-centered, to the neglect of your family and God, both of whom could make you feel better about yourself if you paid them more time and attention.

Whether it's the ingredients to a cake or which friends you spend your time with, balance is always critical. Too much or too little of anything can always be tweaked to give you the right balance you will need in your life. Good balance will stick with you, especially if you learn that little secret early.

Your Heart

Here are two words that are the most attractive to guys: kindness and compassion. I'm not talking about just being nice. I'm talking about what the Bible says about literally being filled up with Jesus, from the inside out. It means that you can be filled up with peace and joy. It flows through your veins and pumps through your heart and invades every part of you. The result is all of those lists that you hear being read at weddings; which is actually this passage: "Love is patient, love is kind. It does not envy, it does not boast, it is not proud. It is not rude, it is not self-seeking, it is not easily angered, it keeps no record of wrongs. Love does not delight in evil but rejoices with the truth. It always protects, always trusts, always hopes, always perseveres."[3]

The reason I started with those two words, kindness and compassion, is because more than any other traits, these two are the ones that guys responded to the most.[4] This was found doing surveys with high school guys to figure out the qualities they appreciated about girls. Guys prefer these two qualities to physical appearance, wittiness, or anything else. For example, let's use a normal, fun, cute, and healthy guy. He might be initially attracted to the hottest girl in the world, but if she is hateful, bossy, self-centered, and unkind to him, I promise it won't last long. The more he matures and the older he gets, the more he will despise these traits and be attracted to the ones like kindness, compassion, and anything opposite to the gross ones.

Physical beauty can be fleeting, but a well-developed heart is what will make a relationship last a lifetime. The more time you spend on matters of the heart—your heart—the more you will be building on something that will be a lasting attraction in your life, and the healthier you will become.

Treasure or Target?

I know you've heard it before, but it's still true: real, natural beauty never goes out of fashion. I won't pretend to completely or even halfway understand the world of girls and how they dress. There are just too many colors and combinations. I will tell you how this relates to guys.

Imagine that you and your clothes are an advertisement. What do you advertise? Do you advertise relaxed, comfortable, cute, or normal? Or do you advertise something else? Maybe your advertisement is about your stomach, your body, your legs, or your chest. Does your advertisement first call attention to your body or to the person inside of it? Imagine yourself as a walking billboard and make sure you know what that billboard says.

The Perfect Body

The way that you act concerning your appearance sends strong signals about how you really feel about yourself. Your ideal body is not a number in pounds. It is not a picture taken and plastered on the front of a magazine. It is about how comfortable you feel in your own skin. It will become more or less attractive to people depending on how comfortable you are with it. Your body is a gift. I'm sure you don't always feel like this and could smack me for saying that so simply. After all, I'm a guy; I have never dealt with bloating or hips or anything else of the sort. But I do know that our bodies are a gift from God. I believe that he wants us to treat them with respect.

How do you feel about your body? You don't have to answer that out loud. But just know that a lot of girls today struggle with accepting their bodies. It seems like everyone somehow believes that there is an "ideal" look that they are supposed to mold themselves around. That is a myth. There is not. You can easily get that impression from hours of television and stacks of "beauty" magazines. But the television and magazines exist solely to get you to purchase things. Turn off the TV and throw down the magazines and start listening to the truth and to reality. Eighty-nine percent of guys are attracted to a variety of girls.[5] We aren't just talking about blondes and brunettes. It also means they are drawn to a vast array of body shapes, body weights, facial structures, heights, and so on. Really, I'm pleading with you to understand this about guys. There are a lot of them. And they prefer different types of people. Most guys don't want a skinny model who struts well. After all, that would look dumb at the movie theatre or your friend's house. Most guys prefer regular walking. A lot of them get fed up with girls who are obsessed with their image and simply prefer a healthy girl. *Healthy* meaning that they are being themselves and not trying to change to look like someone else. The number one answer that I get from guys about what they want a girl to look like is something along the lines of this response: "A girl who isn't, like, obsessed with her looks or always spending a ton of time getting ready. I like a girl who just can relax with who she is and what she looks like. That is more attractive than all the other stuff." While I am not sure there is such a thing as a "ton of time," I do agree with my young friends, and so do most guys.

Go for a Walk

Wanna do something healthy? Go for a walk. Seriously. . . . This will do a lot more than you might think.

A recent study paired individuals in two groups, having one group walk for thirty minutes and the other group rest for thirty minutes. Both groups felt less stress and tension, but the walking group noted higher feelings of overall well-being. Walking has been shown to rid depression and the feelings of depression. In fact, it did this in more than 50 percent of the cases studied; that's more than twice as beneficial as the biggest depression drug on the market. That is more than twice the overall amount that prescription medicine has ever been proven effective with symptoms of depression. The mind will tend to follow the body in many cases. When you exercise, even just walking, your body releases dopamine, which is your body's natural chemical that balances your mood and is the chemical responsible for the feelings of happiness.

Moderate exercise is directly proven to improve self-esteem, relieve symptoms of depression and anxiety, and improve mood. Too much exercise does exactly the opposite. Too little eating will tear your body apart, starting on the inside and eventually working its way out. So don't get confused about the message here. Part of being healthy is treating every aspect of your life in a healthy way.

The National Council on Fitness recommends healthy amounts of exercise. Exercise has an equal amount to do with your physical well-being and your emotional state. Here are some recommendations that are up-to-date:[6]

- Physical activity among children and adolescents is important because of the related health benefits (cardio-respiratory function, blood pressure control, weight management, cognitive and emotional benefits).
- Only 28 percent of students in grades nine through twelve participated in daily school physical education.

- Adults eighteen and older need thirty minutes of physical activity on five or more days a week to be healthy; children and teens need sixty minutes of activity a day for their health.
- Significant health benefits can be obtained by including a moderate amount of physical activity (e.g., thirty minutes of brisk walking or raking leaves, fifteen minutes of running, forty-five minutes of playing volleyball).
- Thirty to sixty minutes of activity broken into smaller segments of ten or fifteen minutes throughout the day have proven significant health benefits.
- Moderate daily physical activity can reduce substantially the risk of developing or dying from cardiovascular disease, type 2 diabetes, and certain cancers, such as colon cancer.
- Daily physical activity helps to lower blood pressure and cholesterol, helps prevent or retard osteoporosis, and helps reduce obesity, symptoms of anxiety and depression, and symptoms of arthritis.

You Are What You Eat

Your body is just like your mind; what you put into it really does matter.

Eighty percent of twelve-year-olds have been on some sort of diet.[7] This doesn't even make sense. Dieting while your body is growing can cause adverse health effects and do harm. Diets are bad; lifestyles are good. A friend of mine in the health industry suggested that roughly 95 percent of diets don't work in the long run. Plus, who likes dieting?

Little changes in your daily diet make a big difference in how you look and in your overall health. Maybe veggies instead of chips, water instead of soda; you've heard all this, right? But guess what, it's true. What you eat will not only affect you physically but emotionally and mentally as well. The good news is that eating healthy is "in." Whatever that might mean . . . it's still good.

> Food for thought: girls who weigh themselves frequently are far more likely to use diet pills and laxatives, skip meals, binge, and vomit according to a recent University of Minnesota study.[8]

Sleep

A lack of sleep can affect your personality, your skin, your hair, and your ability to stay awake and read this book. Many teens get way too little sleep. I know it must be incredibly important to get in a couple extra hours of texting about nothing, but consider sleeping a little more. You probably won't miss out on any giant social thunderstorms. You probably *will* become a little saner and feel better throughout the day. Studies (American Associate for Health Education: www.aahperd.org) recommend teens get at least eight hours, even nine hours, on average for proper health and rest. Don't be the one with your face lying in your drool on the desk in study hall; that's just gross. I've been there. People might take pictures, and some people might like to keep those and make fun of you for years. I'm just saying. This has nothing to do with me and my friend Nick.

Chilax Chick

Basically this is what all of the health stuff boils down to. Relax and take it all in stride. It is about your health. It is all about balance. Take care of yourself. Really . . . not just the outer image thing, but YOU. Take care of YOU!

YOUR EFFORT TO TAKE CARE OF YOURSELF CHANGES EVERYTHING!

A girl who takes care of herself is indicative of someone who likes who she is. It shows that she treats herself valuably. Be conscious of yourself, not self-conscious. This is really what balance is about. Make sure you are thinking about healthy as a lifestyle, not obsessing over it or on just one part of it.

I like Norah Jones's music. It's peaceful and I love jazz piano. It would have been a tragedy if she would have tried to be a runway model instead of using the gifts God has given her. This is true of a thousand other people I know and every other girl on planet Earth. This world needs you being you. God is happiest when you are completely being YOU. We need quiet girls, chatty girls, brainy girls, pretty girls, witty girls, passionate girls, artsy girls, tall girls, short girls, blonde girls, writer girls, piano girls, elementary school teacher girls, doctor girls, and the list could go on forever. There is room for everyone and for all types of girls. There is a guy who loves that type of girl. When you appreciate the gifts that God has given you, other people will appreciate you even more. I think when you use those gifts you are being a witness to the Lord. When you appreciate these things, not only will you grow to be a more beautiful person, but the world around you—and the people in it—will grow to be that way too. Seeing beauty in everyone and everything is the key to seeing your own beauty.

You can never get more beauty until you recognize your own. You are different from every other female on this planet, and somehow you all still share your love for shoes. But you are still different. You have things about you that someone wants to love, cherish, and enjoy. Have you ever considered that one day you are going to be the personification of beauty to a lucky guy? You will literally define what beauty is to him. Make sure you can first define and understand the beauty you were created with.

The last thing is this: stop saying "guys"! What's the point in having one hundred guys like you, or thirty, or ten? The answer is . . . there is no point. Try to keep in mind "the right guy" for you, not just guys! There are lots of different guys, and you shouldn't try to attract them all. When you are focused on your own image, your own morals, and things that have value, you will eventually attract the right guy. That is infinitely more important than simply having guys like you.

I could write a whole book on this point, but I'll try to boil it down. A girl literally becomes more attractive in every way to people when she is optimistic, joyful, and sees God's beauty in lots of places. Health starts on the inside and transforms us all over. Beauty is learning to appreciate who you were created to be.

See, this wasn't so painful, right? And if you didn't like tofu at the beginning of this chapter and still don't like it, then you are just like me. I didn't tell anyone to be on a diet, and hopefully no one will try and smack me or hit me with objects, even if it would be good exercise.

Chapter 6

have only one face

"No one, for any considerable period, can wear one face to himself and another to the multitude, without finally getting bewildered as to which one is true." **—Nathaniel Hawthorne**

If every girl you know is very kind and sweet, then you don't need to worry about reading this chapter. If you, however, are like most girls across the country, you know that sometimes the world of girls can have its challenges . . . especially when a certain type of girl exists: The Mean Girl. In fact, some girls have got this Mean Girl thing down to a science. They are not limited to your high school, your youth group, or even your country. They are everywhere and they are a reality. When I was in Georgia recently, a group of teens told me about a little trick that some girls and moms use to "politely be mean." You just say something bad about someone and follow it up with something nice. Apparently you can be as mean as you want, as long as you start or end with, "God bless her" or something similar. For example, "Well, just look at the way Sarah dresses. It's no wonder people call her a little tramp, God bless her." Or "Bless her heart, you know what she did with Chris after only going out a few times?"

You get the point, right? And maybe you don't use the exact phrase "God bless her," but you or other girls may say something mean and add a "but she does have cute hair" or "but she does dress great." Being negative, putting people down, name-calling, being cruel and harsh, being petty, jealous, or resentful—they are all the same thing . . . mean. However we disguise our actions, these habits can be really harmful. The Mean Girl thing: lots of people do it, but no one likes it done to them.

One of the most common things I hear from teens, especially girls, is how hard it is to deal with Mean Girls. People have been dealing with this issue forever. Throughout the Bible God instructs us on how we should talk. Ephesians 4:29 says, "Watch the way you talk. Let nothing foul or dirty come out of your mouth. Say only what helps, each word a gift." Can you imagine if people everywhere tried to actually follow that advice?

While it's easy and common for us to break people down, God wants us to build one another up. He wants us to encourage, love, and sometimes just deal with the people around us. Doing this in a positive way is something that will be invaluable to you now and for the rest of your life. Learning to deal with people who will be mean is equally important.

Enter the Mean Girl . . .

Here's the plain truth. Guys like girls who AREN'T MEAN! Seems simple enough, right? And I don't just mean to one another, like girl fights, being cruel to other cheerleaders, and other stereotypical teen-movie types of mean. Being mean can include a lot more than those things. Some girls adopt the mean attitude in order to assert power and influence, gain confidence, and get attention. Yeah, guys don't really like that. Well, decent, healthy guys anyway. Is there that one certain guy who is just a jerk to people when he's walking down the hall? Is he someone you're dying to hang out with? Nah. Girls don't really like it when guys are mean.

In fact, they tell me this all the time. Guess what? We don't really like it when girls are mean either.

A lot of girls can take on the Mean Girl persona because they think it will get them something. Maybe it's the sass thing that looks like confidence. Perhaps it's the feeling of being able to say their own opinion out loud, acting like they don't care what other people think. Maybe it's just that they have become self-centered and forget how they are coming off to people (this is common). It doesn't matter what the reason is; it is petty and does nothing for your personality except harm. Let's take a closer look at the mean stuff.

The Mean Teen Queen

Guys and girls have different coping mechanisms, the way that we deal with things. Guys are what we call task oriented. This means that we are driven toward accomplishing tasks. So while girls can be competitive for sure, most guys tend to have this ingrained in their social behavior. This means that we LOVE competition and winning first place. To feel superior guys will outrun, out bench-press, outscore, or outdo other guys . . . in lots of categories. There is an old analogy that explains the difference in how guys and girls will play the "cat" game. By "cat," of course, I mean cattiness, pettiness, and ridiculous stuff like that. Guys tend to want to outdo a guy to feel superior to him. Girls tend to cut the rug out from another girl in order to feel superior to her. In other words, Josh will outscore Richie and feel better; Natalie will start a rumor about Megan to feel better.

The Motive

Have you ever had a rumor spread about you? I'm going to go out on a limb and assume it probably was not an enjoyable experience. Why do you think it impacted you so negatively? Sure, rumors are mean, annoying, and unacceptable, but where does this behavior come from?

Jabbermouth Jenny

Sometimes people get right to our most valuable "resources," our most personal stuff, and those people can be our closest "friends." Have you ever had somebody change something you said, switch it around, make up another meaning, and WHAM BAM, suddenly your friends have turned on you? Well, guess what? I really haven't. Why? Mostly because I'm a boy and that's not a common guy trait. But it is, in fact, a reality that girls deal with. Many girls have experienced betrayal from a friend. They become close with someone they think is a good friend. They share their personal secrets, stories, and struggles only to have the person use the things they learn against them, tell other people, or do other things with information that just hurts.

Subtle Samantha

Nonverbal communication is stronger than actual words. Maybe this girl gives you the roll of the eyes, snubs you a little, and perhaps mixes that in with a little bit of whispery gossip. Then when you actually say something to her about it, she says, "What? Oh, I'm so sorry. I don't know what you mean and I have no idea what you are talking about." Oh please, come on. You know what she is up to, but no one else seems to, and you end up looking like the fool.

Cold Carrie

Sometimes when I playfully want to make my buddies feel awkward I do this move. They might ask me a question and then I look at them right in the eyes and say . . . nothing. That's right, nothing. Then they just wait and eventually start laughing at my weirdness and say something like, "Dude, you are so awkward," and then I say, "Thank you." I am just teasing my friends, but sometimes doing nothing or saying nothing can be pretty loud.

Girls do this too, but for the Mean Girl scenario it is not fun; it is hurtful. Perhaps the Mean Girl ignores you when you say hi. Maybe she talks to everyone but you. This is an effective way to make you feel like you don't exist, to make you feel left out or that you don't have as much value as the other girls. This is a simple and effective tactic because it's all based on nothing happening. You feel uncomfortable and invisible, but she hasn't done or said anything. That's the most frustrating part about the Cold Carrie.

SHOUT OUT

Q: If you want to go out with this guy and he likes you and tells you that, but he has a girlfriend who is your friend and he breaks up with her for you, should you go out with him?

A: Let's reframe the question and look at it from a different perspective. If the guy starts a habit of breaking up with someone for you, who's to say you wouldn't be the girl in the same situation next time? Oftentimes girls can set themselves up for failure by failing to see that a guy who is not that into someone else, or committed, or being a friend, is more likely to do the same to you. Is this the type of guy you would want to be friends with, let alone date? It can often be a sign that he, or you, doesn't have the maturity to commit to things and people in his life. The fact that 94 to 96 percent of high school relationships don't last says that there are more important things here to learn than just your feelings for a guy.[1] You need to learn how to set up friendships and relationships that last and are built on trust and care. It doesn't sound like this relationship would start with those things, and odds are, it won't end with them either.

The other issue here is your friend. Some of the sayings in the Bible are simple, but they make tons of sense. Remember the ol' Golden Rule? Jesus talks about these principles all the time. Treat others the same way you wish they would treat you. Well, just put yourself in your friend's shoes. How would you feel if your friend betrayed you for the attention and affection of a guy? It would feel awful, wouldn't it? Why then would you do that to someone else? Friendship is the single most important thing in any relationship. It means to care about the well-being of others. This is an opportunity for you to do the right thing, and to avoid bad decisions that can turn into bad habits.

There are plenty of great guys out there who will be your friend, build trust by being truthful, and care about you in the ways that you need. You have the opportunity to care about yourself enough to stay away from harmful relationships and friendships. Instead, be the friend you hope someone would be to you.

The Root of Mean IS . . .

If you have ever wondered why these types of things happen, let me fill you in. It's called being cruel, and the real reason is fear, insecurity, and weakness. This kind of stuff doesn't ever come from a confident place; it comes from an insecure one. It is never strength; it is a sure sign of weakness.

The weird part is that even though this pettiness often occurs between girls, it still affects all of your relationships, and that includes the ones with guys. It can affect the way you feel about yourself, the way you feel inside, and the overall interaction you will have in the future with both the guys and the girls in your life. If you let the Mean Girls affect you now, then you will continue letting people do that. If you are mean back, you'll be more cruel and petty in all of your relationships. So what *do* you do?

Relax . . . There ARE Answers

Humorist Josh Billings once said, "There is no revenge so complete as forgiveness." Forgiveness is a sign of maturity and self-respect. Guys like girls who have this quality. The truth is that guys like girls who can rise above this behavior and avoid the rat race altogether. Even if you win the rat race, you're still a rat. That means that if you stoop to the level of this Mean Girl game playing, you have already lost.

Many girls will grow out of this type of behavior later in life when they realize that people don't want to be around them. So you can start by learning to see this ahead of time and forgive people for their behavior in advance. When you see this as insecure behavior, it's a lot easier to not be so affected by it.

Unplug Her Power Cord

When you let someone upset you—especially if you get upset in front of them, as they had planned—you add fuel to their fire. Stop it. I'm not saying to repress stuff; I'm just saying to change your perspective. Hold your own when you are feeling intimidated. Try looking people straight in the eye when you talk to them. This is the best way to let people know that you will not be pushed around. Don't talk too fast or loud, and choose your words carefully. It's about showing yourself respect.

Here's how one girl dealt with Mean Girls. It's pretty awesome.

Olivia Gardner was just another student—that is, until she suffered from an epileptic seizure. Her peers used her seizure to ignite an avalanche of threats, name-calling, and plain old-fashioned bullying that would make her life miserable for the next two years.

Olivia's ordeal was so intense that she even contemplated taking her own life. Recognizing her daughter was in serious trouble, Olivia's mother decided to turn to the media.

Emily Buder, seventeen, and her sister Sarah, fourteen, were listening to Olivia's story and came up with a unique solution. The girls organized a campaign called "Olivia's Letters," so teens could send letters of support and encouragement to Olivia.

After receiving thousands of letters from all over the world, Olivia said on the *Today* show, "I am feeling so wonderful that there is so much support. There are like 100 good people for every bad person there is in the world."[2]

Everything Is a Compliment

A very smart person tells me, every time I see her actually, that I should take EVERYTHING as a compliment. Every comment, every joke, every criticism, and every harsh word someone says to me should be taken as a compliment. And when I stop for a second and think about it, I realize those might be some of the smartest words I have ever heard.

You know sometimes when teachers really get on students about their potential and try to push them to do better? They don't do it to every student. They put their effort into influencing people whom they really see the potential in. So if someone is mean to you, obviously you are influencing them in some way. Instead of feeling hurt, you might consider taking it as a compliment that you are having an effect on a room even just by walking into it. If you take everything as a compliment, I promise you your life will be much happier.

She's Just a Girl; You Are a Girl with Compassion

Realize that no matter how people are acting, God still cares for them as much as he cares for you. It's really sad to see people have to stoop to cruelty and insults to feel better. Stop and realize that people who are mean to others must be hurting. God can use these small moments to fill us with great compassion if we let him. I promise you that when you have the mind to stop and think that way, he really can change your heart, words, and perspective more than you ever can on your own.

In the Bible when Jesus and Paul were beaten by people, spit on, and other terrible things, do you know what happened? I'm sure they had gut reactions to freak out and throw stuff at their heads, but they didn't. Instead, over and over again these stories refer to them having compassion on the people because they saw them as they really were: sheep without a shepherd. They were lost and they needed guidance. If they could do it with people beating them with fists and rocks, I assure you that you can handle that Mean Girl.

Whoopidy Doo

Honestly, in the big picture, who cares? Try to have a bigger perspective here. Shifting your mind first is important. What if you are just being you and some girl doesn't like you, or is being cruel? Do you really want a friend like that anyway? Even if she treated you okay, would you really want a friend who treats other people viciously? Hint . . . the answer there should be NO. Here's a little secret: a lot more people than you realize are desperate for true friends. They are people who will probably make a better friend back too. You'll never realize this until you open your eyes and put out some effort to see this, but I assure you it's there.

Solid Friendships Weed This Stuff Out

As soon as high school is over, the Mean Girl's friends will scatter. I promise you this. I can't tell you how many times I have seen the biggest jerk guys or the snobbiest of girls have a complete personality makeover once they get to college or the work world. The reason is simple. High school is a bit like a prison. Don't tell your teachers I said that. You are forced to go there every day. You can't escape seeing the same people. You are basically forced into a social situation, and there isn't really a way to avoid it. You don't get to choose your schedule, and you can't choose to go ten miles away from people who annoy you. But once you are finished with high school, guess what? You don't have to be around those difficult people anymore. It's just natural for people to like people who are more fun to be around and avoid the ones who aren't. And this will help a lot of the Mean Girls realize that genuine friendships have nothing to do with putting people down but are rather about trying to build them up.

Mean people have been around forever. Even in the Bible you see that people were trying to figure out how to deal with them. Proverbs 16:28 says, "Troublemakers start fights; gossips break up friendships." Gossip can seem like bonding, but it's not. It is creating or basing a relationship on the life or lives of other people.

Do yourself a favor: be ahead of the class, and build solid

friendships now. Do it the right way and not through gossip. It will pay off now and later, not only with girls but in all of your friendships and relationships. This is the best weapon against people who are mean, cruel, or negative to you. Plus, as you invest in the trusting friendships you have with other girls, you will repel the game playing and childish behavior. Working on the solid and caring friendships that you already have, or need to make, is working toward something that can't be broken with bits of insecurity, jealousy, and the ever-present gossip girl.

Whenever we compare ourselves to others, we are bound to think that we should be more this or less that. That's why we can only truly compare ourselves to who God says we are.

Yeah for Honesty . . .

Guys don't like the trick I mentioned at the beginning of the chapter. Girls don't like it either. You don't like it. In fact, no one really likes it. Being mean does nothing but spread hate. Just because you start a sentence with something positive about someone doesn't mean it's okay to finish it with something negative. An easy way to squash out gossip is by asking yourself, "Would I be saying this about her if she was in the room?" or "Is this helping or hurting [insert girl name here]'s reputation?"

Let's recap some of the points we've covered. As you read these, take an honest look at yourself and see how you are doing as a true friend.

- Forgiveness shows maturity and self-respect. A healthy guy will like this quality in a girl—her ability to forgive.
- Don't forget about yourself. Take your own behavior into account. Are you a Mean Girl? The quiz below might shed some light on this. Sure, you may not be "as bad" as someone else, but that doesn't make it okay.
- Take a step back and look at your friends. Are they promoting REAL friendship or are they promoting REAL problems?
- Drama=Goo to Good Guys. If your life is filled with drama, then guys will guess that a relationship with you will be the same way. Stick with more enjoyable activities and less drama.
- Who cares? In the bigger picture it's better to smile and walk away from people who are petty.
- Take everything as a compliment. Seriously try it . . . it changes everything.
- Unplug her power cord. Letting her upset you is giving her control of you.
- Remember, she's a person like you are. God loves

you both equally. This immediately levels the playing field.

- She does it because she is hurting and is not okay with who she is. If anything, this subject is a reminder that people need good, caring, honest, and loyal friends. You should probably be one of those; it works out better for everyone.

Are You a Mean Girl?

1. If a girl in your class got a new haircut which made her look fantastic, you would:
   a. make an appointment shortly afterward to get your hair cut too
   b. tell her you love her new look!
   c. lie and sweetly tell her she was crazy to cut her gorgeous long hair.

2. If you liked a guy, but you knew he liked your friend, you would:
   a. compare yourself to your friend and wish you were more like her
   b. decide to be happy for her
   c. wait for an opportunity to subtly point out a flaw in your friend.

3. If your friends were picking on a girl in the school bathroom, you would:
   a. leave the bathroom
   b. tell them to stop being mean
   c. join in the "harmless fun"

Add up your score:

A = 3　　B = 2　　C = 1

Your results:

8–9

» You may not be mean, but your lack of confidence in yourself can result in you responding in more subtle negative ways to other girls.

5–7

» No, you are not a Mean Girl. You will go so far as to be nice to other girls when it's not easy, and even stand up for the victims of Mean Girls if necessary.

3–4

» Yes, you may not have realized it, but judging by these answers, you could be making someone's life a misery.

Do You?

Do you gossip, do you put down, do you backbite, do you spread rumors, or do you break people down in order to build yourself up? Are you twice as nice as you are negative in your friendships? Most people aren't bad, but they can develop bad habits. The most important thing here for you, regarding both guys and girls, is to make sure you aren't going to be that Mean Girl. There's nothing healthy about someone who is mean. So make sure you are taking your attitude and interactions into account. If you are dealing with insecurity, continue trying to work through it. Insecurity is like a disease, and it's very contagious. The only cure to keep it from spreading is to spread something else: genuine kindness. Kindness toward people is like an impenetrable shield. It's also something everyone wants. People who are mean are often screaming out silently for people to be kind to them. Being kind is so much louder, more attractive, healthier, more fun, more building up, godlier, and more enjoyable than the small and unfortunate pettiness of getting up in the world by breaking others down.

Kindness is in all of us, and it is the surest sign of strength.

Chapter 7

leave us alone

Bubbles

Have you ever experienced the Close Talker, the person who gets all up in your grill when she talks to you? She doesn't seem to understand the invisible line that exists between people. You have a bubble and this person is always invading it. Even if you back up, she keeps coming your way. There is no reason to be examining anyone's breath and teeth at this proximity unless you are a dentist. Well, I don't know about you, but I have dealt with these people. And it is uncomfortable.

There are many ways you can try to deal with them. You can try to move to the side. You can try to sit down on something so that they have to sit too. You can point at something and yell "look" and then run away. You can also just tell them you need a little more space. Personal space exists in everything: our conversations, our bedrooms, our journals, and our relationships.

I like girls. Now you know the truth about me and almost every other guy on planet Earth. That being said, you might find it shocking that sometimes I also *don't* like girls that much. It's not their fault. Sometimes guys just like to be left alone, as I'm sure girls do too. This might be to have some alone time after a stressful day or because a relationship is starting to feel uncomfortable, rushed, or heavy. It's just that in life everyone needs balance. It's important to understand not just that guys need to be left alone sometimes but why they need this. It can be very different from the reasons you might think.

Flip Your Feet Around

You know how sometimes your mom and dad get mad at you and then you all get into an argument? Then finally you have to go to your room just to get away and you don't want to deal with it anymore? Why are they always on your case? Then your mom stands in the doorway of your room and tells you that she won't be disrespected and goes on about how you need to listen to what she says and there are so many other things on your mind that you just want to scream, "LEAVE ME ALONE!" Okay, well, that's not really what this chapter is about. But you can probably recall some similar scenario where you wanted to scream that.

Now let's flip things around. I always draw up scenarios where the guy becomes the girl or the girl becomes the guy for a moment, just so we can try to see how the other shoe fits. Plus, it's always a good way to see how our behavior and opinions can be interpreted by the opposite sex. At some point you will feel like you want to scream, "Leave me alone!" to a guy. This might be about some guy, one guy, many guys, or all guys, at some point in your life. Why? The reasons can vary, but consider the following scenarios:

You have two boys who catch your eye. Which one of these looks more appealing to you?

Guy A

Guy A is a Clingbot. There is no doubt that he digs you big-time. In fact, pretty much everyone knows this. He calls and texts like it's his job, only he's not getting paid for it. He wants to shower you with compliments and talk about you TO you all the time. Clingy guy looks at you all the time, runs over to your locker and talks to you every chance he can get. He gets you gifts even though there isn't really a reason for it, just to prove for the hundredth time how much he likes you. He wants to know if you feel the same way about him, but usually he wants to know this daily, and he keeps asking you about it. When you are at a friend's house and some guys come over, you know he is going to head straight over to you. He smothers you with the obviousness of how much he is into you.

Guy B

You can't tell whether or not he has interest in you. You want to know, but you can't quite tell. He doesn't play games, but you find yourself wanting to know more about him. He seems like a well-rounded guy. He plays sports, has a lot of different friends, has some cool hobbies, and you don't see him at all social occasions like other people. Maybe he's interested in dating; maybe he's not. You may not be quite sure, but you know he is really normal and nice and doesn't look like he's desperate to be in a relationship. He seems pretty happy. He's kind of curious . . . or at least that's how you are about him.

So, Guy A or B? I'm guessing B, right? Okay, now imagine that YOU are one of these guys. If you could only be one of these guys, which one would be more like you? Are you more like the obvious Clingbot? Or are you a more self-sufficient, balanced, not-dependent-on-the-other-sex-to-fill you-up type of person?

Of course not everyone fits into just one of those two boxes, but they would be MORE likely to fit into one of them than the other. If you are in the first one, you may want to slow down and reconsider things a bit. It's important to see how we can be viewed by other people. It's not ALWAYS a bad thing. It can give us a third-party perspective, and this helps us to see ourselves through other people's eyes. Do you look more like someone who would be well balanced or would you look like the Clingbot?

And who wants to be a Clingbot? My guess is not you.

Boy Friends and Boyfriends

I'm sure you know that it is important to have some time alone. It's also good for guys to have time alone. Here is a little hint: guys tend to be better boyfriends when they have boy friends. Read that carefully. It just means that it's important for guys to have guys in their life even when there is a girl. A lot of teens don't do this well. More often, a guy wants to spend all his free time with a girl he likes, or a girl wants to spend all her free time with a guy she likes, rather than striking a balance. Too much candy will give you cavities. Sorry I just sounded like your dad. But it is true. Too much of any good thing often spoils that good thing. As hard as that can be at times, it is important to learn that balance.

This is Alex's story that he shared with me:

Megan was pretty cool. I was on a ski trip with our class, and Megan and I ended up skiing a lot together. I always thought she was pretty cool, and we had been friends for a while when we started going out. I started to get a lot of feelings for her. At first it was great. I liked taking her out and laughing. We would always have a good time. Then after about a month things started to change and take a turn. I have always had a lot of buddies, and I like to do a lot of other things too. Megan wanted to spend all of her time with me, and it kind of started to bug me. Then she would text me constantly and it was like she had to keep in contact at all times, and it started to happen all the time, which I wasn't cool with. I mean I liked her, but I also liked other things in life too, not just her. Every time I would tell her that I was going to spend more time doing other things with my friends or at sports, or even my family, she would start saying, "Fine, I guess you just don't like me as much as I thought," and "Well, if a guy likes a girl then he spends all the time he can with her." I don't agree with that stuff, and it wasn't long until I decided to stop seeing her. My feelings went away for Megan. I didn't want them to, but they just did. Instead of liking her, I was trying to hold her off and trying to constantly tell her that I did like her but I like to do other things besides just have a girlfriend. Why did she have to do that? I don't get it. I think if she would have relaxed it would have been better. She didn't have hobbies or that many other good friends either, and I think that's another reason why. Now I think that would have made a big difference. It stinks too because she was really cool, but she was just too into me and our relationship. Stuff like that has to be balanced, you know? Anyway, I just wanted to write to say that since we were talking about relationships and I can totally relate.

—Alex M., 16 years old, California

Back to the Boy's Brain

Our brains are different! And, boy, does this become obvious when it comes to the time we spend with one another. Remember spaghetti and waffles? One of those waffle compartments might be "our relationship." That doesn't mean that we are always in that compartment. It means that when a guy is with his friends, or at soccer practice, or playing guitar, or shooting off fireworks, he isn't necessarily thinking about a relationship with a girl. Both sides of the brain tend to work simultaneously in girls. They may think about several things more naturally; for instance, a guy and homework at the same time.

The misperception for many girls is that if a guy isn't thinking about them as much as they are about the guy, then the guy doesn't care about the girl as much. This isn't necessarily true. It means that guys prefer to think about, spend time doing, and invest in one thing at a time. It also means we have a harder time singing, patting our head, and texting at the same time compared to you.

So, don't worry if it seems like a guy isn't always thinking about your relationship. It's normal, it's natural, and it's also healthy.

Back to the Wilderness

One of the most important things I have experienced is learning to enjoy my time alone. Not all guys like being out in the middle of nowhere, but I sure do. I'm not alone in this either. I know a lot of guys and girls who would agree.

For a few years in a row I spent the summer in either Alaska or Colorado. I have an infatuation with Alaska still. I remember every moment of time there. The summer breezes blowing through all of the tall grassy fields are a sight to see. The strange, crisp smell of the ocean that only exists in the far Pacific Northwest will haunt your senses. You can never forget this smell. The mountains spring straight up out of the water and soar high above the valleys and plains to create breathtaking beauty. Sometimes I would be on an island by the shore with a fishing pole and no one else around for miles. I would stare up at the blue summer sky with my feet in the freezing clear water and just take deep breaths of pure air. I spent a lot of time outdoors, sleeping in the woods, eating strange stuff, and NOT concerning myself with girls. I'm not saying this is for everyone, but I did learn a lot of things because of it. One of those is that there are so many great things in life. One of those is relationships, but there are so many more than that.

Abraham in the Bible spent a lot of time in the wilderness. He not only became clearer about who he was, but he also became clearer about who he was in God's eyes. The same thing can happen with us, and we don't have to go out in the middle of nowhere to understand this. (It may help, but it's not necessary.) The time we spend doing things alone—or at least outside of a relationship—can really help define who we are, what we like, and what we don't like. It's difficult to do this if a relationship takes up all of our time. And it was Abraham's image, confidence, and leadership that he developed spending time alone that surely added to him being a good husband, a father, and the biblical legend that he is.

A healthy guy's image is not found in girls. Likewise, a girl's image is not, and cannot ever be found, in a guy. We are so much more than just somebody's girlfriend or boyfriend. And we can never be a whole person if we focus solely on relationships. We need our own image, and we need to spend time learning what that image is. When girls give guys space to do that, they end up with much higher quality guys in return.

Look Around and Learn

Do you know a girl who seems to be obsessed by the idea of relationships with guys? Maybe she has always jumped from boyfriend to boyfriend. Maybe she spends all of her time thinking about guys and all of her free time texting, IMing, writing about, flirting with, doodling pictures of . . . GUYS. You might be this girl, you might be friends with this girl, or you might avoid this girl like the plague.

Now here is the real question: does this obsession help or hurt her?

Seriously, does she seem to have herself more figured out or less figured out because of this?

Does she seem emotionally stable or more up and down?

Does she understand guys more or less when she constantly envelops herself with guys?

Does she seem clearer about life and relationships or more uncertain?

If you examine these questions honestly, you might reconsider how much time you want guys to take up in your life.

I WANT and I NEED

Ben and Kari were now officially "boyfriend and girlfriend." After going on several dates, Ben talked to Kari about just seeing each other, in other words, being exclusive. They were both excited. Kari loved Ben's independence, and Ben loved how much fun they had when they spent time together. As time went on, though, what seemed great began to be not so great. For one thing, Ben's independence turned into distance. Kari loved the independence and strength that Ben displayed, but her need to spend time with him was too great. She began to call him more and more, which pushed Ben to display even more "independence." She always wanted to know what he was doing, and every time they chatted on the phone or on IM she would tell him that she missed him, even if they had been around each other that very day or the day prior. She tried to plan for them to spend a lot of time together nearly every day. Eventually, she began to distance herself from her friends and adopted Ben's as her own. For Ben, things got equally uncomfortable. He really did value time with Kari, but he also valued time with his friends and family. The more Kari tried to spend time with him, the less he enjoyed spending time with her. Ben felt suffocated and confused, and eventually learned that he needed a girlfriend who was fine with spending time with her friends without him, had a separate life, and didn't seem so dependent on him.

This could have been the exact opposite story as well. Ben could have smothered Kari, and she would have wanted to get away. It happens a lot, and it's because of a simple thing. There needs to be a balance in all of our relationships. Sometimes there is a difference between things that we want and things that we need. Kari wanted to spend a lot of time with Ben. What she didn't understand was that people have different needs, and it's important to respect those needs.

Do you think about the things that you NEED from someone you would want to spend time with? It doesn't mean you want a boyfriend right now or anytime in the near future. It just means that you are thinking ahead of time about some important stuff.

make a list

Things I Want in a Guy

Things I Need in a Guy

Now, compare these lists. Are there any differences here? I'm guessing confidently that there are. Preferences in the opposite sex are like an outfit or a car. There are things we *want* to have—like sequins or a sunroof—and things we *need* to have—like sleeves and a steering wheel. And the point for you is to have at least SOME idea about those things ahead of time. That way, when the right or wrong guy comes along, you're better prepared to see how he fits into your wish list. You will be better prepared to handle the relationship. It's like studying for a test ahead of time but WAY more enjoyable than studying. You can be sure that these lists will change over time. And you can keep track of them and see how you change as well.

Respect Our Space and We'll Respect Yours

The issue of time and space in relationships all hinges on respect—showing respect to both people. Respect is one of the most important things in any relationship. And it's important to respect the other person's need for space, as well as your own.

One of the most important things for guys is to feel like their time, their space, their abilities, and their possessions are respected. Just giving him the space he needs is a simple sign of your respect for him. This works both ways. Make sure the guy has enough respect for your space as well. Disrespect, clinginess, and possessiveness have NO place in a healthy relationship or friendship. Respect is just one of those ingredients necessary for things to work right.

What if You're Not the Clinger?

If you think I'm just preaching about you girls being clingy and needy, hang on. Many girls know that there are versions of the male Clingbot too. For the sake of both you and the clingy guy, it's important to set appropriate time limits. I'm not saying you should bring a stopwatch, but just consider healthy chunks of time. Don't feel pressured to spend more time with someone than you are comfortable with. Your time is valuable; don't just give it all away.

Ask yourself these questions:

- How many nights in a week is it good to see someone?

- On a given night, how many hours do you think it's normal to hang out?

- How much time each week do you leave for yourself? (Remember how important that is!)

- Do you both like to spend the same amount of time together?

As you review your thoughts and answers, think about how this compares to how much time you *actually* spend in your relationship. Are there any ways in which you need to adjust the time you spend with your boyfriend or friends? If so, stop thinking about it and make a plan now to make that change. Your image, your personality, and your social life will give you a big high five for it.

Why Is This Important?

This whole topic really has a deeper meaning. When it comes to teens—or anyone, for that matter—an imbalance can mean they are missing out on something else in life. If you are always concerned with guys, odds are you are not leaving time to develop in other areas of your life, like friendships, education, and future plans.

God has a lot more planned for your life than for you to worry about whether or not someone likes you or if someone knows that you like them. He has already chosen the perfect guy and the perfect path for your life, so obsessing over guys really is just a waste of your time. He also wants us to spend time with him. People can easily get wrapped up in one another and forget who should be the real guide in that healthy relationship—God. God wants us to care about one another, but he wants us to grow closer to him as well. Be sure to leave room to nurture the most important relationship ever—your relationship with God.

In a lot of ways I think our relationships should directly resemble God's care for us. If your dad says that you are going to spend "quality time together, whether you like it or not," something happens: obligation. Instead, I think God wants us to encourage one another, to be giving and not selfish, and to care and love freely, not out of obligation. The best way to do this is to make sure that while we can enjoy one another's company, we can also enjoy the company of a lot of other things and people in our life.

There are too many girls who are now women, moms, and professionals who didn't realize the importance of striking a balance when they were younger. Many of these women wish that they had spent more time growing themselves into a more well-balanced person than concerning themselves with guys. They tell me this all the time. There is a whole lot more to life than just dating. Take a moment to look past the crowd of guys and see what else is out there. You will find something better than guys. You will truly find yourself.

This life requires balance, and I hope that you will work to find it.

Mystery Chat Quiz

1. If a guy likes a girl, what do you think he tells his friends?
   a. something like, "She's really great!" and that's it
   b. nothing
   c. everything a girl would tell her friends about a guy she likes

2. What do you think guys talk about most when girls aren't around?
   a. girls
   b. school
   c. common interests

3. What do you talk about most when you're with your girl friends?
   a. guys
   b. school
   c. common interests

Answers:

1 = usually a 2 = c

Chapter 8

have a life

"I like girls that are well-rounded, but you know in a good way, probably not in the way I first thought of. I mean the personality stuff, you know?" **—Some kid who made Chad laugh**

You may have read this chapter title and said, "What?" But when's the last time you took a break from life long enough to examine life itself? If you answered, "Um, never," it's okay. You're just like most other teens—and many adults. Yet if you want to get a real life, a quality life that is full and balanced, you've really got to take a moment to step back and look at your priorities in life and the way you're living it. It can take a long time to achieve that full and balanced life, but it's never too early to start.

A great girl is far more than the sum of her shopping, her hair, her nails, her clothes, and her makeup. So first, let's take a look at your priorities. Take a moment to number the following general life priorities in order of importance. And there isn't a perfect answer. It's your life and your priorities.

_____ Education
_____ Family
_____ Work, chores, household tasks
_____ Clothes, makeup, shopping
_____ Health, fitness
_____ God
_____ Friends
_____ Guys
_____ Helping others
_________________________ (other)

Next, let's take a look at your life. Take a moment to look at the last week and jot down the things you spent time doing. Start with the things you spent the most time doing and on down the line.

Now, if you were to put the first list and the second list side by side, how many of those things would line up? For instance, if God is your number one priority, is that the thing you spent the most time on last week? I know school is mandatory, and you are required to spend a certain number of hours there, but that should really be the only exception. Otherwise, how do your priorities line up with reality?

How can you begin—starting today, now!—to live your life based on your values and priorities? Rip out this page, post your priority list on your mirror or bulletin board, and live by it. I don't mind . . . go ahead.

"Clothes? You put them on, and then you wear them." —Michael, 14

On the list above, what priority did you give to clothes, makeup, and shopping? And how much time do you actually spend thinking about, talking about, looking at, picking out, debating over, trying on, and twirling in clothes? Clothes and makeup (and shopping for them) are both part of your overall body image, which we all know can be a normal, healthy thing. But many girls fall into the trap of worrying about these things too much in order to improve other people's opinion of them, especially guys'. When these things are out of proportion in your life, they become an unhealthy burden. They can shape your personality, and they can negatively influence the way others see you, guys included.

Studies show that the average woman will look in the mirror more than seventy times a day. That comes out to one time every thirteen minutes that you are awake.[1]

While clothes are good, especially if you don't want to get sent home from school, they can also be a huge distraction. So . . . if I may ask you a question . . . are you distracted? Seriously, do you buy shoes because you need them, or because you need them to define you? Do your outfits, your hair, and your looks become something that's a normal part of your day or a distraction that takes up entirely too much of your time and your mind? Perhaps it's time to start weeding out some of these distractions and shoo away the fly in your ear telling you to obsess over these things.

> "If I'm looking at a 'cute girl' I'm never wondering if she'll play basketball with me, but the 'girl next door' would, and that's who I want to spend time with." —Ryan, Virginia

Being of the male variety, I'm probably not a very good judge of the importance of clothes in a girl's life. In my humble opinion, more than thirty minutes spent in range of a dangling price tag is deserving of a psychiatric evaluation. But if you think you may be a bit too worrisome about your appearance, first, it's good that you're aware of that. And second, see what you can do to adjust for the better.

Try doing something you'd never normally do. Try NOT dressing up for school one day. Or, if you want to start small, ease up on some of the makeup you usually wear. Making yourself a bit uncomfortable by doing stuff like this can help keep you in check with reality, and also help you grow. Plus, you'll learn that others will still really like you, even if your purse doesn't match your blouse that day.

Anthony: Hey, Zach, do you want to talk about shopping, or our hair, or our nails, or our outfits?

Zach: Sure, man, I would love to never ever do that.

Okay, I'm going to tell you something that might rock your world. I have heard that there are some guys out there who don't love the following things: shopping, doing our hair or thinking about it, anything to do with our nails except knowing they are all still there, and spending time thinking about what we are going to wear, especially picking out something to wear in advance. Don't get me wrong; there are plenty of guys who do think about some of these things some of the time. And when I consider the ridiculous amount of "product" for your hair these days that grants us the ability to spend lots of time looking at our heads in the mirror from different angles, spending time on your hair is even understandable. However, even with cool hair products in place, the majority of guys don't spend nearly as much time thinking about their looks as girls do. Is this a shock to you? Probably not; me neither. But it does have to do with both the way you see yourself and the ways guys see you.

One factor to consider is, do you want to look good, or do you want to look good for guys? These are two entirely different things. What tends to be more attractive to guys is when you worry about these things because you enjoy looking good and want to be healthy, not because you want our attention.

Some of you might disagree. Your past experiences with guys might tell you otherwise. Some guys might seem to be obsessed with looks, and if you've experienced this first-hand, it's no doubt had a real effect on you. Maybe a guy broke up with you or a friend of yours because he was more interested in girls who dressed and acted provocatively. Unfortunately, these experiences come from guys who aren't healthy and well balanced.

> "Sometimes I get frustrated with my girl friends. I like that they make efforts to take care of themselves, but like, how much time do you need to spend doing it? When we are hanging out, they obsess about how they look and what I think about it. I wish girls would just relax."
> —Chris, 16, Minnesota

The truth is that guys, even high school guys, tend to want a girl who isn't concerned about constantly looking good for guys. This always comes up in our conversations. They prefer to know, be friends with, and date girls who have that part of their life balanced. That means they want a girl who cares about taking care of herself, but not to the extent that she's just taking care of herself in order to please others. To us, that's just completely out of whack.

Consider this example about Zack. Zack was pretty comfortable with himself. He wasn't the kind of guy who was too confident or too shy, and he was great at playing guitar, which he knew Kelly loved. He and Kelly had been dating for a little while, but it was still in the not-that-crazy-serious stage. Zack loved hanging out with Kelly whenever they had the time, most of the time at least.

What started to confuse Zack, and sometimes even made him feel uncomfortable, was how much time Kelly spent worrying about how she looked. There was never a day that they'd hang out when Zack didn't have to help Kelly decide what to wear. First she'd start with the jeans, usually giving him four or five options, trying on each pair, and then slowly narrowing it down. He always wondered why someone would own so many pairs of pants. Then it was on to the shirts, the necklaces, and then the shoes, oh my gosh, the shoes. She must've gone through her entire wardrobe every time they'd go out. When he'd ask her about it, she'd reply, "I want to look pretty for you." But Zack got the feeling that wasn't really the case. She never seemed happy with how she looked. When she'd come back from going to the bathroom, Zack could count on her making a comment about how awful she looked. Her nose, her stomach, her eyebrows, her butt, something was always wrong with her appearance.

When she would talk about whatever it was that day that she hated about herself, it was obvious that she wanted Zack to interject and tell her that it wasn't true. Kelly would constantly fish for Zack to compliment her. This was something that Zack wanted to give her, but Kelly's lack of comfort with herself made him uncomfortable too. He always wondered, "Why can't she just be happy without worrying about all this junk? She obsesses over it. It's weird. I don't think it is good at all."

Whether or not Zack could describe it in words, he was turned off to Kelly. Her obsession with her self-image and her outfits and her desire to be affirmed were things he realized he couldn't handle. He might not be able to describe this in depth, but his instincts told him that she has unresolved issues that he could not solve for her, but would get in the way of having a healthy and fun relationship.

Have a Life Quiz

1. When you get dressed, how much of your outfit has to do with guys liking it?
   a. 80% or more (You tend to wear cute little T-shirts. *It's only right to celebrate your best physical attributes. Isn't it?*)

b. 50% (You wonder if that new guy in English class will notice your cool, new sneakers.)

c. 20% or less (The only time you think about guys noticing your clothes is if you've spilled something on the front of your oversized sweatshirt.)

2. How many parts of your body would you change (if you could convince your dad to pay)?
   a. at least one
   b. none
   c. three or more

3. How often do you feel good about how you look?
   a. most times (You look hot in like everything.)
   b. sometimes (You feel happier when you wear your favorite jeans and shirt.)
   c. almost never (You wish someone would sign you up for a TV makeover.)

4. If you went out without makeup on, what would be your worst fear?
   a. guys being repulsed by you
   b. scaring yourself when you look in the mirror every thirteen minutes or so
   c. girls looking down on you

Add up your score:

A = 3 B = 2 C = 1

Your results:

10–12

» It seems your life revolves around guys—trying to impress them with how good you look.

7–9

» You "have a life"—a healthy balance of wanting to look good, being willing to live with the body God gave you, and a good sense of humor!

4–6

» Judging by your answers, your life revolves around hiding underneath an oversize sweater hoping not to draw any attention to yourself.

You're Laughing at Who?

Do you like a guy who walks around all the time puffing his chest out trying to act macho? Or would you like a guy who seems way more comfortable with himself, even to the point where he can laugh at himself?

Right, most people would pick the second option.

If you want to know what guys like about girls, consider this: we all like someone who can laugh at themselves. In fact, it's one of the most charming traits of some girls I know. I certainly have never heard a guy complain about a girl who was able to laugh at stories about how she was goofy or embarrassed, or any funny story about something dumb she has done. In fact, I think most guys would say this ability is kind of important.

To me, people who can laugh at themselves are hilarious. Who doesn't want to be around someone who can tell a story about themselves that involves them being flawed? There is almost nothing that people can relate to more than that. Who wants to hear about your perfect skin and how you've never made a mistake in your life? Not this guy, because most guys like people they can relate to.

My friend always used to tell me, "The only certainty I have about life is that I'm not going to make it out alive." He made it clear that he always wanted to laugh and make sure that he was enjoying whatever came at him in life. My point? Don't take yourself too seriously. All of this self-examination can be tiring and even discouraging sometimes. Being able to laugh at yourself while still being able to appreciate who you are is a great place to be.

Dodgeball Dummy

I don't usually like gym class anyway; that's what makes this story

just awful. I like to play the sports that I enjoy, not the one my bored gym teacher tells us we have to play, and that includes dodgeball. Of course all of the guys love dodgeball to death, and last week in gym class I finally decided to play with everyone else. I stayed in the games longer than usual and I guess just the intensity of playing caught up with me, but I really, really got into it. Seriously man, I flipped out and kind of got in the ball-throwing zone. I started throwing the balls at anyone who came near the center line, and that included three of my teammates. I didn't even know I was hitting my own players until everyone started yelling at me and booing. I single-handedly lost the game and everyone was laughing at me. I think I'll be picked last in everything we do in gym class from now on . . . . Lol. I think I'll just take up yoga or something that I don't hit people in the face doing.
—Mariah, Connecticut

I wanted to share some of the stories that I have had the pleasure of hearing. So may I say thank you for sharing your stories with me and now everyone who reads this book? If you have other stories, send them to stuff@chadeastham.com.

Whatever You Do . . . DO

So, it's Friday afternoon, last period, and you're talking with your friends about what's going on that evening. What's a question that is usually going to pop up every time? Probably something along the lines of: "What are [insert boys' names here] doing tonight?" If you do a little digging, you may be surprised to see how much of your activities can revolve around guys. Now, I'm not being conceited, and I'm certainly not complaining. But since we are on the subject of balance, we might as well consider it. How boy-motivated is what you do?

The Nothing Text

6:30: Jenna—"Hey Lexi, this is Jenna. Just wondering what you were gonna do tonight. Are the guys going to go out to eat like they said or what? Text me and let me know what's up. Kisses."

7:04: Lexi—"hey. just out of shwr. call u soon."

7:23: Lexi—"Hey. I'm not really sure what's going on. I'm waiting for Rob to call me back, but I am hungry. I have to dry my hair and get ready. My brother keeps barging into my bathroom. I'll see what's up."

Jenna—"Okay, I'm still getting ready too. I'll see if I can get any of them to answer their dang phones. Call Amanda too. She said she wants to hang."

8:10: Lexi—"Yeah, Rob hasn't called me back or responded to my text. Neither has Chris."

Jenna—"Gaahhh. I don't even know why they have cell phones, it's not like they ever answer them."

Lexi—"I know, right? I'm starving. Let me finish getting ready and I'll call you."

Jenna—"K."

8:32: Lexi—"anything?"

Jenna—"no. this is dumb"

Lexi—"im ready whenever. I'll just come over.

Jenna—"k"

8:58: Jenna—"hey. rob just textd me. they got a pizza and arent doing anything except playing night basketball or whatever. Still comin' over?"

Lexi—"almost there. Whatre we doin?"

Jenna—"dunno. Nothing I guess."

Sound familiar? I'm sure something like this has happened to you, and if not it probably will, although I hope it doesn't. Don't let inactivity be your only activity, just because the guys aren't doing anything. We may not be the best at keeping you up-to-date on what we do do.

Whether it's going shopping, tanning, getting your nails done, or as in the above example, just doing nothing, how much of this stuff do you do for the sake of us? Honestly, do you ever stop the noise and think about this?

Is it 100, 90, 75, 50, 30, 15, 0 percent? Many teens don't typically stop to evaluate the motives behind their actions, or to figure out what portion of them is for other people. Do you think your percentage is good and healthy, or does it need to be toned down?

Now flip it. How many conversations do you think guys have with each other about how to look, what to wear, how to wear it, and what to say to make girls pay attention to them? Some guys, not the majority, actually do this a lot, but it probably isn't the best use of their time.

How many times have you heard guys say something like, "You know what, Steve? Forget about girls tonight, man; let's just get the guys together and go out and go shopping!"

That sort of thing probably happens once in a never . . .

Do healthy guys, or even most guys for that matter, spend lots of time thinking about how they look to you? Excluding prom and wedding days, I would say, no, not too often. What would you think if one of your guy friends spent as much time as you may spend, worrying about how he looked in his clothes, his ashy complexion, or how his hair just wouldn't agree with him that day? My guess is you'd think he's a little strange. Consider that the next time you ask us for the thirteenth time if those jeans make you look fat.

Okay, Chad, so it's good for me to spend time with guys, but it's not good for me to revolve all of my activities and motivations around the "boys." Well, that's neat. So what am I supposed to do instead of that?

I'm glad you asked. Great question . . .

For starters, why not have a GNO (Girl's Night Out)? You know how every girl hates a "catty" friend? Well, they're usually "catty" because of boys. Take the boys away from the evening, take away the drama.

Play with your dad's video camera and make music videos (friendly note: don't let this video end up on the Internet; it can get creepy), make a fort out of pillows and blankets and have an indoor camping night, rent a bunch of movies and make brownies, start a Bible study that doesn't involve figuring out guys, or develop a hobby that allows you to create value and beauty without the boy drama.

Then, maybe take it a step further. Reach out beyond guys and your circle of friends by doing something great in your community. Ask your church pastor, a teacher at school, or a parent for some ideas. Check out www.idealist.org. Those are great places to start, and the less recognition you get for doing nice things for people, the better. Remember, it's about them, not you.

These girls got super-creative with their free time and ended up changing the lives of others!

- Haley T., age eleven, donated her hair for cancer last year!
- Shauna Fleming, age eighteen and from Orange, California, started an organization called "A Million Thanks," sending over two million thank-you letters to troops in Iraq. She even got to meet the president of the United States!
- Michelle H., a girl who was diagnosed with a life-threatening disease, was given a trip to Paris from Make-A-Wish, and decided to donate her art and raise money for the organization.

Doing good things for other people will help you overcome your own fears and insecurities, realize humanity, and create gratitude. There's really nothing more fulfilling than doing something selfless for someone else.

So, get a life. A real life. A life of balance, confidence, health, and generosity. When you figure this out, you'll be way ahead of the game. And in the end, you—and the future guy of your dreams—will thank yourself for it. There is something really important and healthy about a girl who cares about looking good because she wants to be healthy, and not because she simply wants to look good for others. The first way works for your whole life; the second way will always leave you buying more junk to fulfill something that can't be bought by junk.

I'm not saying shoes are junk; in fact, I'm not even going there, but you get the point. Having a life that is truly yours is as important as oxygen. I'm fairly sure oxygen is as important as shoes.

Chapter 9

can spell

Hooray for the Alphabet

There's a good chance if you are reading this that you have learned the alphabet. You also know that letters are used to spell words. There is one word that you should learn to spell. It might be the most important word you ever learn. It's not hard, so I am sure that you'll be able to do this. This word will be with you your whole life, and it's spelled like this . . .

N . . . O . . .

Try saying it out loud. Repeat after me, class: NO. Learn this word and your life will be much easier. In this particular case, this word isn't negative . . . it is completely a positive thing. The meaning of the word *no* creates a boundary, probably one of the clearest, most important boundaries that exists. It is also one of the hardest to learn. Still not convinced that this little two-letter word is that important? I'll share with you one reason.

Scared Little Me

I have walked home at night, alone, and in the dark. I have been afraid. I don't mind admitting it. In fact, I have been afraid of many things. These include, but are not limited to: alley cats, strange windy noises, puddles of water, paper bags, Bigfoot, and other strange mythological creatures that I know don't exist.

One thing I have NEVER feared is this: while walking home by myself in the dark, a girl was going to be hiding in the bushes, then when I wasn't looking she would jump on me, knock me to the ground, and then proceed to take advantage of my body. This is not a fear, never has been, and it never will be. When I mention this fear to a group of guys, I'm usually met with a crowd of smirks and smiles. They do this because this scenario is not a fear for guys; it's usually a fantasy. Guys are a lot more likely to dream about this type of thing than they are to be afraid of it. When it comes to pressure, physical aggression, and the nature of who usually is the chaser and the chased . . . it tends to be the guy who is in the bushes.

Learning to Say NO!

How many times have you heard about a girl who has been put in an uncomfortable situation? How many times have you heard of a girl going further than she was comfortable going with another guy? How many times has someone compromised their own values, limits, and morals because they were uncomfortable confidently saying no? The answer is . . . A LOT!

The national statistic for girls who are in some way sexually assaulted in their lifetime is one in four. Twenty-five percent of all girls walking down the street experience this awful pain.[1] Both their bodies and hearts are assaulted and sometimes may never recover. They experience first-hand the worst in people and pay a price for other people's sin. This is NOT their fault, so hear me say that loud and clear. There are many reasons why these things happen. Some of them are unavoidable: a father, a family member, date rape, or something else that you have little or no control over.

Sometimes, fortunately, these uncomfortable, boundary-breaking situations CAN be avoided when you own the meaning of the word *no*. Learning to say no confidently in your life would probably drastically change the number of times girls are negatively pushed beyond their limits. It's heartbreaking to see someone experience this type of thing. Do not become a statistic. This word, and the meaning of this word, can help people from experiencing some of these horrific pains.

There is a reality for us in the world. We need boundaries.

No . . . I am not your dad. I'm not your mom. I'm not here to tell you what to do. However, I will say that boundaries are important. But they are also a really positive, good thing. A lot of teens might think about boundaries like they are just rules. They are not. They aren't negative, they aren't bad, and they aren't about constricting your ability to have fun in life. When it comes to your personal boundaries, you should reconsider them as necessary, positive things. I want you to think of boundaries, as some people like to say, as though they are the cheese to your macaroni. And if the girl is cheese and macaroni, the ingredients of boundaries and freedom have to be added carefully, in the right amounts. Do you know what the right ingredients are?

NAME 10 HEALTHY BOUNDARIES IN A RELATIONSHIP WITH A GUY.

1.
2.
3.
4.
5.
6.
7.
8.
9.
10.

NAME 10 THINGS THAT ARE NOT OKAY IN A RELATIONSHIP WITH A GUY.

1.
2.
3.
4.
5.
6.
7.
8.
9.
10.

You don't have to write these down, but please take a minute to consider the answers to these questions.

- Why do girls often find themselves in uncomfortable and compromising situations?

- Can you list five boundaries girls tend to have a hard time setting with guys?

- Why do some girls give in to the pressure from guys to do things that they later regret, while other girls do not?

- Aren't boundaries about keeping dogs in the front yard and children from running across the street and getting run over by a bulldozer? First answer: not in this book, weirdo.

- Why is it usually girls who feel more pressure to compromise in relationships than guys do?

Your Front Yard

Have you ever had to mow the grass in your yard? Isn't it strange to think that people stop mowing the grass at an imaginary line that separates their yard from the next? It's called a boundary. You can't see it, but it's there. Have you ever given thought to what a boundary actually is? What does that term mean to you when you think of it? And besides that, what purpose does it actually serve?

Well, in the case of your front yard or your bedroom door, it serves as a line. It's almost like a property line, isn't it? There is a different kind of line too, and this one is yours. It distinguishes what is your property and what is not. It's pretty noticeable when someone has crossed over into our own personal space. Someone puts their hand somewhere that you don't feel comfortable with, maybe they put their face too close to yours, or maybe they start asking questions that are too private and you don't want to answer them. Usually we don't like it when people invade our personal space, and we need to show people the line that they have to stop at. Like a front door, people need to knock on the door and get permission before they are allowed to see what's inside. These are our boundaries, and they usually serve two functions.[2]

The first function is to define who you are. They are a notice to yourself and others about what you like and don't like, what you will accept and what you won't, what we like and what we hate. Boundaries tell people how far or close we want them to be. These boundaries exist ALL the time and are usually easier to notice after people cross them.

The second purpose that they serve is to protect you. Basically they tend to help keep the negative stuff away, and to attract the good stuff more naturally. Have you ever heard the saying "If you don't know what you stand for, you might fall for anything"? Well, it works like that here too. Boundaries are there to protect your reputation, your body, your and other people's feelings, and your most valuable asset: your heart. How many girls have you known who have exposed their bodies and their hearts in the wrong way or to the wrong person? When you don't have these boundaries, you are much more likely to expose yourself to harsh elements. Just as a coat is a boundary between your skin and cold weather, your personal boundaries protect the innermost (and sometimes outermost) parts of who you are.

Awkward Little Experiment

Try this. I call it "getting up in people's Kool-Aid." Walk up to someone but stop around five or six feet from her. As you are talking to her (make sure you look her in the eye), step three feet closer to her. After another few seconds move two feet closer to her so that you are about one foot away from her, maybe even a little closer than that. You can observe some good reactions. Most importantly, you will notice that people will want to get away from you. You are too close, and they don't feel right about it. It's also funny and awkward, so feel free to vary up this little experiment and practice it often.

Training Wheels

You will probably find that when it comes to the opposite sex, for both of our sakes, things go better when they are defined. If you are clear about your morals, your preferences, your limits, and your own values, it helps to solve a lot of potential misunderstandings that can come if you don't. Boundaries are like the training wheels on a bicycle. They help guide you. If you jumped on a bike for the first time when you were a kid without any training wheels, you would wreck. Trust me, I have scars to prove it. The training wheels help us gradually get the bike moving more smoothly and without hurting ourselves. The same is true with boundaries in your personal and dating life. The more you know these things about yourself, the easier it is for people to know these things about you ahead of time.

Kristen

Kristen has started dating. Her friends know her reputation. She isn't going to jump into a relationship. She isn't going to get physical with the guy she is seeing, and she is only interested in guys who are going to treat her respectfully, never pressure her, and know that she has a lot of other things in her life that take up her time. She is only interested in a fair and balanced person whom she will do things with occasionally. She is also serious about her spiritual life and is more attracted to someone who shares the same values and perspective on faith that she has. Not only does she do this for herself, but these are the signs she is wearing so that other people can know who she is and who she is not. These are some of the things that define who she is, they are natural boundaries, and they will help her when it comes to relationships with guys.

I don't know about you, but I'd say that Kristen is a smart girl. She knows where she stands, and she knows what she stands for. It is you and only you who will define these boundaries for yourself. I have dealt with a lot of young people who let themselves be controlled by others. Whether it is your emotions, your feelings of love, your limits, your time, or your set of values, it is bad when you leave it up to other people to define these.

Dating Is a Reality

Dating is a normal part of the socialization process, as long as there are healthy boundaries. Why is that, though? Dating and relationships do have risks. It doesn't mean you shouldn't be interested in the subject, but it does mean your maturity will many times determine the outcome. As Dr. Henry Cloud says, "By its very nature, dating is experimental, with little commitment initially, so someone can get out of a relationship without having to justify himself much. Putting lots of emotional investment into a relationship can be dangerous. Therefore dating best works between two responsible people."[3]

It's kind of hard to argue with that reasoning. It's also hard to think it's not important to make choices based on your values and your understanding of what dating means. Healthy boundaries are the single best way to have fun, and to grow in your relationships, enjoy freedom, maybe the love stuff eventually, and become encouraged about guys . . . not discouraged.

Let me give you a couple of examples.

I remember the day I went to buy my first car. It was a pretty sweet SUV, and it made me sixteen inches taller instantly. It smelled like happy. But buying a car can be tricky. Getting hassled and hustled, arguing prices, and learning about the different cars are just part of the process. However, I did know one thing. I knew exactly how much I had to spend and about how much car I should get for that amount, and I was given the advice that I should be ready to walk away if I wasn't comfortable with the situation. If I hadn't planned ahead, I probably would have been pushed around.

There was one car salesman who would have taken me for everything I was worth. He started pressuring me, and after I got back from test-driving the car, he tried to get me to sign the paperwork for this car immediately! It felt like a bad deal. I felt the pressure, didn't like it, and simply said, "Hey, I didn't say I was trying to buy a car right this moment, and I don't like you trying to pressure me to." Know what he did? He said, "Well, I've got other things to do, man, so whatever," and then he walked away. Pretty rude, actually. It could have been worse, though . . . I could have been unprepared for the situation and could have caved to the pressure.

I walked away two separate times before they gave me the car, and I got an amazing deal on it. Go me!

The point is, of course, not to teach you how to wheel and deal on car prices. Understanding boundaries will help you with car shopping and, of course, boy shopping. Planning ahead, setting boundaries, and knowing your limits before you walk into situations usually will result in a happier ending.

A Less Dude-ish Example

I had a date once in high school. Not just one date, okay, but I'm trying to make a point here! My buddy had started seeing a girl and she had a friend so we decided to double-date. It was the fall, football season, so we had Saturday nights free.

During this time in my life, I was actually at a really healthy point in my friendships and relationships with people. I didn't really want to date around a lot, I didn't want to get in over my head, and I wanted to respect myself as well as other girls. I also didn't want to drink, especially since I had just had some problems with that in my life. I basically had in mind that I was going to go have fun and hopefully make a new friend. I really didn't feel like trying to make my first date with someone all romantic. Call me crazy, but I wanted to have fun.

Well, it didn't really go like that at all. And, boy, am I glad I decided a few of these things ahead of time. The girl was pretty much the opposite of me at the time. She was really focused on herself, talking about her car, how much money her parents had, pretty much all night. She just wanted to go drink and took every opportunity to point out that if we were drinking it would be more fun. She was really unpleasant to be around all night. Don't get me wrong, I wish her all the best and hope she grew out of it, but the date was dumb.

As she kept pushing the drinking thing, I finally said, "What's the big deal with drinking? Are you that miserable with us that you just have to drink to make it bearable?" She didn't know what to say. Then she acted annoyed and tried to treat me weird for not thinking beer is the coolest thing on earth. Oh yeah . . . I should mention that she wasn't dressed very well either, meaning that she was promoting her body more than her personality the whole evening. This didn't help either of us.

I finally got sick and tired of the whole thing. I simply told her that I wasn't having a good time and that I was just going to head home early. She didn't like that very much, but guess who didn't care? That's right, this guy.

Girls like it when a guy has set boundaries, plans, goals, and morals for himself ahead of time. Not all girls—like the one in my memorable date—maybe, but the ones he wants to be around are able to appreciate that about his personality. They may not even always know that they like it, or say it out loud or anything, but it makes it a lot easier to be with someone who has some rules and guidelines written into their personality. For example, the guy who kind of shows in his actions that he isn't going to try to take advantage of you, or pressure you in conversation, or make crude sexual implications, or make fun of other people when you're hanging out is someone who is easier to be around than someone who isn't. Get what I'm saying?

The same goes for the other side. Guys like girls who have some of this stuff figured out. Not all of it, it's a learning thing, but at least some of it. Plus, it's kind of the natural "weeding out" process, isn't it? What your actions and morals say is inviting to some people and off-putting to others. But I can promise you this . . . trying to plan ahead, setting boundaries in your life, and planning out some scenarios, especially with guys, will make this whole guy/girl thing go a lot more smoothly than if you are just "winging it."

Are You a Boundary Setter?

1. If a guy you were hanging out at a party with made complimentary, but inappropriate, remarks about your body, would you:
   a. feel uncomfortable but tell yourself to grow up and take a compliment?
   b. enjoy the compliments because "there's no harm in words; he's just a typical guy"?
   c. politely tell him he's being inappropriate, ask him to stop, and go talk to someone else?

2. How do you think drinking alcohol would affect your ability to say no?
   - **a.** depends on how much you drink
   - **b.** you would still know what was right and wrong
   - **c.** it could make you a little more lenient and adventurous

3. If you and your boyfriend are in love, and you know you are going to get married, is it okay to sleep with him?
   - **a.** you've never thought about it before
   - **b.** you're not sure if this is right or wrong
   - **c.** you have a clear opinion on this

Add up your score:

A = 3   B = 2   C = 1

Your results:

8–9

» No. You are often not even sure of what is right and what is wrong.

5–7

» Definitely not. You are too lenient in potentially dangerous situations.

3–4

» Yes. You know what the boundaries are and have the will to remain on the "right" side.

Take Heather for example:

"Wow, those paintings are great!" Heather was really impressed with Tim's art. Maybe it wasn't so bad that she went to his house after all. Yeah, she didn't know him very well, but Tim seemed like a nice guy and was a REALLY good listener, something Heather thought was nonexistent in the realm of boys. She had thought twice about coming over—Tim's parents weren't home, but gosh that smile! It made her giggle just thinking about it. I mean, after all, they both had to study for the same history test the next day, so why not? "I have some more art upstairs," Tim said.

Okay, something didn't feel quite right about this. Heather's stomach turned a little bit, almost telling her not to go up. She shook it off, telling herself that she was just being silly. She followed Tim up the stairs, swiping his leg to make him trip and stumble. They both laughed as he tried to recover. Ahead of her, he turned the corner and jumped back around, as if trying to scare her but wrapped his arms around her instead. "I have really wanted to hug you all day," he said.

No harm in a hug, Heather thought to herself, even though this kind of caught her off guard. She hugged him back, and they stood there for a moment, embracing each other. Several seconds passed until Heather said, "We should probably get started studying." Tim let go of her, saying, "Gosh, stop worrying about it. We have plenty of time. I have some more stuff I want to show you." They walked down the hall to his room. He had a poster of her favorite band on his door! He opened it and walked in.

Heather hesitated for a second. Things still felt kind of weird. Her parents would kill her if they knew she was at a boy's house while his parents weren't home. Not only that, but she was about to follow him into his room. He grabbed her hand and pulled her in.

He showed her around, pointing to more of his art and some of his baseball trophies. He must've been to twelve different countries around the world. There were so many pictures and foreign objects on dressers and shelves. He sat down on his bed and watched her pick up a picture of his family, pointing to his siblings. Beckoning her to sit by him, she brought the picture over. They laughed about how much he looked like his mom. And then it happened.

One moment they were laughing about his family, and the next, Tim was hugging her. "I love the way you hug," he said to her. "And your hair smells so good." He laughed and put his hand on her leg while his other arm was still holding her. Heather took his hand and moved it off her leg. He was still hugging her and put it right back on her thigh.

This had gone far enough. Heather pushed Tim away and told him that she was getting a bit uncomfortable with all of the hugging. Tim scoffed and said she was just being uptight. "No, I'm not," she said. "I came here to study with you, Tim. It's not that I don't trust you, but your parents aren't home and I am not comfortable with you touching me the way that you have been. I know that you can respect that."

"Fine, geez," Tim said. Embarrassed, he got up and tromped out of his bedroom and down the stairs. Heather could see that Tim was not interested in studying after all. She packed up her stuff, told him she was just going to study at her house, and left.

Much like guard rails on a windy road, boundaries are not meant to be pushed. Instead, they can keep us from being hurt, hurting others, or even hurting ourselves, especially if things get out of our control.

Your Job

Your job is not to please a guy. Your first job is to protect yourself. One of the easiest ways to do this is to get comfortable using that word *NO*! It clearly defines limits, and it is a natural way for you to build confidence in your own decisions. This doesn't just apply to the physical limitations of boyfriends and pushy guys; it goes way beyond these things. This applies to who you let into your life, how much you let them in, the types of friendships you'll have, and the amount of self-respect you are confident in showing to yourself and to others.

Successful Women

Is there another girl whom you really look up to? Perhaps she is a little older and has had more experience in relationships than you. I have met quite a few people in the last several years. When it comes to the girls I have met, there is a certain quality about many of them that I can pick up right away. Girls who seem to have successful friendships, relationships, careers, marriages, and everything else seem to share a common trait. They don't have a problem saying no. It helps define who they are. It defines the confidence they have in their own beliefs and boundaries. And you know what else? People respect that about them. You don't have to be old to have this confidence. I see it all the time in high-school-age girls and guys. This makes their lives a lot easier, and it usually helps them enjoy their friendships and relationships more too.

Here are some questions for you to answer to find out if you are confident in saying no:

- What are some situations you don't have a problem saying no in?

- What are situations you DO have a problem saying no in?

Hard to Get . . . Easy to Respect

I mentioned this earlier, but it bears repeating: guys like to work for stuff. Or at least I should say that we appreciate things more when we have to work hard for them. So when it comes to your friendship, your time, your attention, or your affection, how hard do people have to work in order to gain access to you?

This isn't a game, and you shouldn't play one when it comes to your friendships or relationships. However, I've noticed that when it comes to girls who appear really valuable, another trait pops out. They aren't easy to get to. Girls who typically attract healthy guys aren't that easily accessible. In fact, it seems like the more they value themselves and therefore the more discerning they are about who they let into their hearts, the more it tends to weed out the unhealthy guys, and to attract the healthy ones.

This isn't a numbers game. It's far more important to attract quality to your life over quantity. The more you value yourself in healthy ways, the less accessible your heart is to lots of people; and the more you define who you are and who you are not, the more you are increasing your value. Here is a hint: everyone has value, but it's up to you to spend time appreciating it, developing it, and learning more about the unique person you were created to be.

Access to You—Difficult or Easy?

1. A good-looking guy at the children's summer camp you're working at is flirting with you, but you're not sure you really like him. Do you:
   a. enjoy the attention and flirt back?
   b. be friendly, but make sure he knows you're not interested?
   c. enjoy a harmless summer "fling"? Someone good-looking is better than no one, right?

2. If a cute new guy comes to church, and you like him, do you:
   a. without saying anything, make sure he (and everyone else) "knows"?
   b. keep it to yourself (and your sworn-to-secrecy

best friend), and wait to see if he shows any interest in you?

c. tell your friends in the hope that they will spread the word and he will find out?

3. If suddenly, during lunch break, all your friends had to leave the table and you are left alone with a guy you have a crush on, would you:
   a. get panicky, desperately think of something cool to say, and hope he doesn't make an excuse to leave too?
   b. make the most of a great opportunity to speak to him one-on-one and get to know him a bit better?
   c. put your flirting skills to the test?

Add up your score:

A = 3   B = 2   C = 1

Your results:

8–9

» Access to you is difficult in the negative sense. You send out the wrong signals making it difficult for guys to read you.

5–7

» Access to you is difficult in a good way. You don't

throw yourself at anyone and don't jump at the slightest attention paid to you.

3–4

» Access to you is easy in a bad way. You try hard to get attention and affection from guys, whether you like them or not—as if it's just a game to see if you can.

No Fear

Most of the time when people are apprehensive about setting strong limits there is one main reason: fear. Whether it's the fear of rejection, or humiliation, of awkward situations, or any other reason, our fear can be the breaking point in our confidence. The Bible says that God provides for the birds and other creatures of the earth (see Matthew 6:26). Are we really afraid that he isn't big enough to provide us with what we need?

Have you ever really thought about that passage? Sometimes we can be afraid that someone won't like us anymore if we don't give them what they think they need. Sometimes we really want people to like us, and we don't like to see them upset. Sometimes girls fear that someone will not love them if they aren't willing to show the other person the type of love that they are pressuring them for. No matter the circumstance, do NOT be afraid. God loves you; he backs you up. He cares about you and encourages you to respect yourself. That is what saying no is about. It's about showing yourself enough concern to refuse the things that aren't good for you.

Happy God

God really does desire for us to be happy. You don't tell a little kid not to play with the electrical outlet because you want to bum him out. You do this to protect him so he doesn't lose a hand. God wants to protect us so that we can be full of happiness, clarity, joy, and peace. He wants us to trust him. When we set our eyes upon pleasing him, suddenly pleasing others pales in comparison. He doesn't always say this will be easy. In fact, it can be really difficult at times, as I'm sure you know. But I have found that most of the great things in my life, including my friendships and relationships, have had their struggles. But far and away, being confident about boundaries and self-respect was the clearest way to work through them. Learning to say no is the simplest shortcut to a clear understanding of your limits. It is not just a barrier. It opens up all of the things you should be saying yes to. Saying yes to the good things is way more fun.

Remember, in Spanish, that's "no." Shall we move on?

Si.

Chapter 10

can high-five and punch

"I like girls who can, like, punch you and stuff, but they also smell good. It's good when they can do both of those things." —**Ben**, 16 years old, really likes girls

There is a word that guys sometimes say about girls. In most contexts, it's just a simple word, but when guys use it to describe a girl, it is different. It is special. Guys may use it to refer to a lot of things they like, but when they use it in reference to a girl, the word becomes slightly deeper, slightly more sacred, and more difficult to explain, the word is . . .

Cool.

Since I wrote my last book something really cool happened. I got down on one knee on a beach in front of a girl and said some important things. Then I took out a ring and asked my friend of ten years if she would be my wife.

I don't usually look nervous. Even in front of thousands of people I talk pretty normal and I don't get too worried about things. When I go skydiving or surfing or boxing, I don't even get nervous about my parachute not opening, a big wave owning me, or someone knocking me out. Yet when I was on one knee looking up at a smiling brunette on a gorgeous beach, I was beyond nervous. I tried to keep my cool about me, but my heart was thumping about eight feet out of my chest. It was the most nerve-racking moment I have ever had in my life. Apparently this was good because she thought it was cute and girls like it when guys get nervous sometimes. A big man who can punch me really hard does not make me nervous; a five-foot-five brunette with the power to choose between the words *yes* and *no* can bring me to my knees . . . quite literally.

One of the reasons I like Laura so much is because I know who she is. I have known who she is for years. That's the benefit of friendship. You usually get to know someone better as a friend than you do if you just have the romance goggles on. I not only knew the great things about her, I also knew the hard stuff, the struggles, and the mistakes. I have this stuff too, and luckily, I could relate. It's comforting not only to relate to someone who is as fallible as you but to also watch them grow and learn from their humanity. In fact, it's probably the most comforting thought when you decide to spend your life with someone, the fact that you are already their best friend.

It's amazing and ironic how much girls will worry that they are going to just stay a friend to someone and they will never find romance, when in fact it's usually the opposite. Being real friends without motive is probably the best formula there is to begin a relationship. To me, it simply means caring about the well-being of someone else first, more than anything that I might want. I always cared deeply about Laura as she did about me. Laura being my friend was the single thing that attracted me to her the most.

Then, there I am on one knee, looking at a little brunette asking her if she likes me enough to marry me. Lucky for me she said yes. She said yes at the altar too, which made it official. So now we travel a lot together, I have to clean up my stuff more, and she has to try and tell people her last name is Eastham not East Man. Normally I wouldn't talk too much about myself or my personal life, but there is a reason why I am now. Laura and I met in our teenage life.

We were friends when I was sixteen. I thought she was ridiculously cute, and I suddenly, but quietly, was hoping something I did would catch her eye. I was wondering if a girl like that could ever like a guy like me. Apparently she did, a little bit at least. She just never really told me. I never really told her too much either. Instead we did something that was probably better—even if you roll your eyes at me—we became friends.

The reason I say this is because you know what friends do? Stuff . . . that's what! Stuff! They do things together. Forget romance for a moment and think about all that it can keep you from. Climb a tree, go caving, play basketball, volunteer together, ride horses, go to Mexico to help people, or just sit and talk for hours and hours. I have found that sometimes a quick romance can get in the way of activities that actually help you learn about someone.

Okay, okay, I won't go off on a rant here. I will simply say this: Do you know what I like about my wife the most . . . the absolute most? This includes the majority of the time, more than I think about romance or kissing or all that stuff?

I like that she is *cool*.

That's how I think about her. Of course I think she is beautiful. However, I can do more with someone who hikes than I can with someone who is just pretty. Luckily she does both of these things well. I think to myself in a guy voice, *Man, I have a really cool wife. I seriously like her.* Now of course, love, romance, intimacy, and all the gooey stuff is important too, but it doesn't take up the majority of your time with someone. What ends up being the most helpful for dating, for marriage, for hanging out, for intimacy, and for anything else to do with guys and girls seems to be this: it's really important to know how to be a friend. It's very hard to like someone whom you wouldn't first consider a good friend. It might take some people awhile to figure this out, but most people come to this conclusion at some point.

My wife likes to do just about everything. She is up for all kinds of new things. She'll jump out of a plane, eat weird food, backpack in Thailand for a month, live on a bus with me, go snowboarding, go exercise with me, teach me how to sketch, or become friends with anyone who will be a friend back. While that isn't necessary or important for everyone, it is to me. My buddies talk about my wife and they say, "Dude, your wife is great. She's really cool, man, that's awesome." This comment, by the way, is like the Mount Everest of comments about girls from guys. Guys may talk a lot about the way girls look, but when it comes to spending a considerable amount of time with someone, you quickly find that looking at someone doesn't make up for the fact that you actually want to enjoy their company as well. It's why we like our friends.

I like that she is my friend. This is the foundation for everything else in our new relationship. I guess I do like that she'll punch me just to tease me or if I get out of line, and yet she still smells good. I guess I actually can see the point that kid with the goofy quote at the beginning of the chapter was making.

All right, enough about me; let's get back to you.

You're Normal? Great!

Don't underestimate the value of being pretty normal. What I mean is, for guys, the word *normal* is really comforting. Teenage guys especially do not like highly stressful social situations. So when things are pretty normal, for lack of a better word, we are more comfortable. We like less stressful and more normal.

Normal can be vague. Here are a few answers to what guys said that they like about girls in social settings. Please excuse their grammar and incomplete sentences.

"Girls that are pretty cool to just kind of talk to, and can hang out and just kind of . . . do stuff together."

"Sometimes in a group when girls are there it means that the guys might do other stuff than just give each other a hard time."

"I don't know man why are you asking me this stuff? It makes me feel weird."

"I dunno guys usually just kind of sit around and don't always talk a lot, and I guess girls kind of make more stuff happen when you're with people."

"I like how girls are really excited and positive. At least I think they are anyway, they seem like it. They're more excited about stuff than me."

"I like girls that are your friend and stuff, and aren't always thinking about like dating and all that stuff."

"They always ask us questions, and I guess they make us talk about things and our thoughts and other stuff than just movies and video games. I guess that's cool, I like that, most of the time anyway, except when I want to not talk about that stuff."

"They like to make food and cookies, is that good? I think it's good. Actually I think it's great."

All right, you get the point here? I have so many more answers like that where those came from. The funny thing is how, on average, uncomfortable guys are expressing their thoughts on the subject. I would almost say it's really cute, but I won't, because of course . . . wait, too late. Oh well, I spend a lot of time around girls.

Guys generally like girls who are natural, comfortable, and don't change the social situation that we are used to. These are the words that keep popping up. I mean, the more normal you are, the more you are like a friend. And we like friends. We are getting comfortable with ourselves as well, and that is why one of the most common questions I get about guys is: *Why do guys act differently when you're alone than when you're around other people?*

Around the country girls are asking this all the time. In fact, it might be THE one question I hear the most. And it's a great chance to learn something about guys and our sometimes curious behavior. I know your teen years can be just as complicated as guys' can be. But know that it is quite a journey for guys to be comfortable with themselves too.

Do you have your entire personality figured out? Neither do guys. That's the simple answer. In fact, guys' emotions and their logic aren't working as simultaneously as yours do right now. That means that teen guys often separate their social life and romance easier than girls.

Guys also get hounded by other guys. A guy especially gets a lot of grief when he's glued to his girlfriend when other people are around. Considering that guys do care what other guys think of them (even if they don't seem like it), they might form two different-looking versions of a boyfriend: the private boyfriend and the public boyfriend.

There are lots of guys on planet Earth. There is no one type of guy. I've seen a lot of serious PDA-loving guys, and plenty of the type of guys who keep a careful distance in public. Perhaps one way to think about it is by imagining that some guys can have different "modes." Sometimes when there are other guys around, you just don't necessarily want to be in "boyfriend/emotional/handholding mode." Just like you can have different moods, a guy can have a hard time figuring out how he is comfortable acting from one situation to the next.

While it's confusing, the less time you spend trying to figure this out, the better off you might be. I know this isn't often what some girls want to hear, but give the guys a few years; they will develop. Perhaps slower than you might like, but the right ones will develop at just the right time.

The best thing you can do is set standards for yourself. That way the guys in your life have a better road map. As a guy it's also comforting to know that I can just be myself around a girl who is comfortable with herself, and then this whole process of "how to act" goes much more naturally.

Even though Tessa had lots of boy friends, she had never actually had a boyfriend. In fact, most of her friends were guys. She hadn't really planned it that way, but she just seemed to get along with guys better than she did with girls. Out of the few girl friends she did have, Stacie was her best friend. They hung out a lot and were friends with a lot of the same guys. However, Tessa was really confused about how guys treated her compared to how they treated Stacie. Like there was that one time that Stacie burped while everyone was out for pizza. Everyone acted like it was really cute and funny, but when Tessa burped a few weeks before that it was "GRROOOSSSSS!" Tessa had always been the girl who got called to come over and shoot hoops, or to run errands with at the mall. Guys came to her for girl advice, and it was often advice that involved Stacie. Even though Tessa was much closer to the guys and they spent more time with her, it bothered her that they thought everything that Stacie did was so funny and precious. She was only asked to dances "as friends" from guys while Stacie would go on a real date! Was Tessa doomed to forever being thought of as "just one of the guys"?

Maybe you can relate to this story. Don't worry. This is actually pretty common, and lots of girls have talked to me about similar situations. Some feel they will never be looked at as more than a friend and others can't understand why they are the receiver of friendly pestering. Whichever situation you may find yourself in, it's not a bad thing, and something different from what you might think is probably going on.

You remember the stuff about guys liking social situations

that are normal and comfortable to them? A big part of why you may feel "doomed" to friendship or forever being picked on is because these are the types of interactions guys are most comfortable with. If you're the friend, it's because guys are comfortable with you and LIKE TO BE AROUND you. They come to you for advice because they don't feel comfortable asking her.

By now you're hopefully starting to realize that high school relationships don't typically last long or end well, and because of that, there is a really easy and fun way to go about the whole guy thing. If you're like Tessa and guys come to you for advice and to hang out, or just generally seem to enjoy your company in a non-romantic sense, then this is a good thing. It means you are trustworthy, liked, and approachable. It gives you lots of room to see what type of guys you like to be around and to make some good decisions about the types of friendships you want.

Everyone Wants a Friend

I was a pretty shy kid. I'm actually still pretty shy, believe it or not. In fact, it's really uncomfortable writing about things that have happened to me, my personal story that is, which is why I'm kind of forcing myself to do that a little more here. While a lot of other kids start high school by jumping on the bus, grabbing their books, and going to class, I did not.

Instead, I was sitting in a long-term detention center. I always forget that a lot of people don't know this about me. Like I said, I tend to talk more about things than I do about myself.

I was a pretty confused and messed-up kid. I am slowly becoming normal, thank you for your concern. However, I didn't feel very normal for most of my life. I, like a lot of kids, didn't know what normal was, tried quietly but desperately to fit in, and strived to have friends. I think most of us do that, and it seems like pretty natural behavior, in fact. Nothing I did really worked, though, because of one simple thing: I thought that I was just too different. I thought I was a loser. Even though people who knew me didn't think so, it didn't matter because I had a hard time believing anything good about myself.

Maybe it was my family situation. We didn't have a lot of money. Maybe it was all of the moving around, new schools, and new situations that I wasn't capable of handling very well. Whatever it was, I made some bad choices. Like a lot of teens, I looked for acceptance, normality, and care by being a rebel. I don't mean it in a cheesy way, like I was wearing a bandana and a black leather coat; I just mean that a chaotic-feeling kid will reflect that in his or her behavior. After all, we live out our emotions. I had a lot of frustration, insecurity, and anger about life, and being rebellious was the easiest and most natural way to show that I was confused.

I also got really confused with my habits. I bit right into

the alcohol apple, thinking that it made me look a little bit older, a little more confident, and a little cooler because I was being different and "doing my own thing." With that, also like a lot of other teens, came the introduction to drugs and to people who weren't developing good habits either. Within a very short time, my grades bombed. I became consumed with things that felt good quickly, and I stopped planning, or being able to plan, for the future. Have you ever noticed this? Almost all things that feel good, taste good, and look good immediately don't turn out very good for us. When it's quick and easy, it's usually harmful.

Before I knew it I was sitting in a small room with couches, surrounded by a bunch of guys who were ready to tackle me if I flipped out. I found myself in a long-term rehabilitation center for teens. I remember everything about that moment, that day, and all the days that followed. I, of course, felt more hopeless and like a loser than I had ever felt. I couldn't even be a rebel. I was in drug rehab, and it felt like I failed at that too.

I spent several months fighting, arguing, and lying to myself about the problems I had to face. My biggest dilemma was that I simply didn't think I was very valuable. This simple fact, my friend, can be a big and ugly monster in a person's life.

It wasn't until several months later that I finally broke down. Thanks to the help of some friends and peers, as well as great counselors, I finally gave up on trying to keep it all together. I finally took a deep look inside myself. I didn't like what I saw. It took a lot of crying (turns out guys can do that . . . go figure) and a lot of healing and encouragement to see that a lot of people feel like I had felt. Most importantly I learned that I was far from hopeless.

Little by little, I made a few jokes, cracked a few smiles, thought about other peoples' situations, talked about what I thought about myself, and expressed my feelings a little more. I started to believe that there might be hope. I realized that I could go back to my life and that there was still plenty of time to straighten things out, start anew, and lead a pretty normal and happy teenage life.

After about seven months of being in that program, I was finally allowed to go back to school. This was a huge step because it forced me to go back to a school and be around other "normal" people. It was weird. I had a lot of rules, I kept to myself, and I had to learn to interact with people in a way that I had never done before. But you know what helped me? A couple of guys and girls changed the course of my life. A few of them stick out in my mind, and they are still friends to this day.

Enter Two Chicks

Math class, yeah. Geometry is a blast; I'm sure you'll agree. But I liked geometry because something took place in that class that was more important than learning the cosine of a triangle: Kasi and Sarah started to talk to me. Kasi would turn around from time to time and do something really weird and normal. She would just kind of . . . talk to me. It almost didn't make sense to me. She was a cheerleader, very cute, and very much someone I wouldn't be comfortable initiating a conversation with.

The thing I remember is how relaxed she was with just saying hello and asking me simple questions. She remembered my name and said things like, "Hey, Chad, how are you?" Then she asked me where I was from, and it just kept going. Her friend Sarah started talking to me too. I realized in geometry that this girl and her friend just wouldn't stop being genuinely nice. It almost freaked me out.

So how is going to school here? Are you making any friends? So what kind of stuff do you like to do outside of school? Do you have any brothers or sisters? Do you have this math stuff figured out, or do you need some help? There were lots of other normal questions, and both girls seemed like they enjoyed talking with one another and talking to me. They didn't treat me like I was strange; they treated me normally. They seemed to overlook my awkwardness knowing that I was a new kid and I probably didn't know many people.

It was my first interaction in a long time in a normal setting with girls. They helped me to feel really comfortable, mostly because they were nice and seemed to care what I had to say. They weren't being pushy, or being super loud, super outgoing, or super anything. They were just being kind human beings. And guess what? I really liked that. It helped me. It helped me to open up a little bit in conversation, it helped me to feel free to voice my opinion, and I felt like people actually were genuinely interested in what I had to say.

This was incredible. What I am saying is that, as a guy, one thing that means a lot to us, whether or not we actually say it, is when girls are pretty normal. Normal meaning they tend to just talk with us in a very relaxed tone about life, school, and all the day-to-day stuff. You may never know how much that means to someone, but I assure you, it does mean a lot. Guys may not always come out and say this in gratitude, but it's extremely comforting to talk with someone who is genuinely interested in being nice and is interested in another human being.

Those two helped me open up leaps and bounds not only in class but later on throughout high school. They were some of the first people who showed me that talking and just having buddies could be cool, fun, and normal. It was a no-pressure situation talking to them, and it turned out that I enjoyed it. If they weren't there and hadn't been so normal and nice, then I might have had a completely different experience in both that class and everything else that I encountered that year.

I can't tell you how monumental these relationships

were to me. My whole high school experience, my friendships, my college experience, my after-college experiences, up until right now sitting here typing this sentence have been affected positively because of that small gesture of kindness she showed to me. Last year I sat at Kasi's wedding reception and watched her pledge her love for her new husband. It was really cool. She probably won't ever even understand how much of an influence and how helpful she was in my life. She did something pretty astounding, and yet pretty normal. She showed God's love as a friend. She was genuinely interested in who the new guy at school was and helped him to feel a little more comfortable.

Never underestimate how God might be using you in someone's life. You can't go wrong by being a genuine friend. You don't know their story and how you might be helping to shape it in a great way. I am so thankful for those two people letting me know that it was okay to "be me" and that there were people who were genuinely interested in me.

At the end of the day friendship is the answer to a lot of the questions we have about one another. If you want to have a good relationship, learn how to be a good friend. If you want a relationship that is healthy, positive, mature, fun, and God-centered, then learn how to be a friend. Friendship is not selfish; it is caring. Friendship protects us, it keeps us safe, and it safeguards our hearts and emotions until a great friend comes along and earns a place in our hearts that is special. Friendship is the most natural and necessary way for us to learn about one another, and God really wants for us to understand each other. He opens up his hands and gives us friendship so that we can.

Chapter 11

lol & ttyl

What We Say; How We Say It

Three weeks. THREE WEEKS! It was late Saturday morning, three weeks before prom and NO ONE had asked Jennifer yet. It was beyond embarrassing to hear everyone talking about prom and she was the only one without a date. Well, at least she felt like she was the only one. Meredith, Susan, Kari, Stephanie . . . the list went on and on in her head. All of her friends had been asked to go by some pretty cool guys. Was she the only one left?

She rolled over in her bed and looked at the clock. Ugh. It was 8:00 a.m. and she was wide awake. *Might as well get up then*, she thought to herself. She went downstairs and was greeted by an empty kitchen and a note from her parents saying they had to run some errands and would be back in the afternoon. Opening the fridge, she scanned the shelves looking for something easy to make for breakfast. Next it was the freezer. There it was . . . Mint Chocolate Chip Ice Cream, her favorite. *Might as well start my day with some healthy dairy*, she thought. *It's not like I have a prom dress to fit into*. Without getting a bowl, she grabbed a spoon, plopped on the couch, and flipped on the TV, her comfort zone.

DING-DONG! That stupid doorbell made her jump every time it rang. "Coming!" she yelled as she hoisted herself up. She opened the door and no one was there. Confused, and kind of offended that she was the brunt of someone's cruel ring-and-run joke, she turned to walk back inside and noticed an envelope on the doormat that had her name written on it in fancy silver letters. She picked it up and opened it to find its only contents were a small key and an address. What was going on? She ran inside and jumped on the computer to Google the address. *That's weird*, she thought, as she noticed it was a post office box.

She threw on her clothes, grabbed her keys, and ran out

the door. She found the box at the post office and opened it to find two pieces of paper. One said, "You" and the other said, "Southside Mall . . . Fire Hydrant . . . Red Balloon." Was someone watching her? Was this some kind of joke? She looked around but didn't recognize anyone, and no one seemed to be paying her any special attention. As she pulled up to the front entrance of the mall, there it was . . . a yellow fire hydrant that had a red balloon tied to it. She grabbed the balloon and could clearly see two more pieces of paper in it: one with the word "to" and the other with another location and something to look for.

This little scavenger hunt she was sent on by a mystery someone continued on to several other places, eventually leading her to the wishing fountain at Eden Park with six pieces of paper that said, "Will you go to prom with . . ." The last clue instructed her to look for someone carrying a red umbrella, which was odd because it was completely sunny outside. Rounding the corner there he was.

Scott Webb was sitting on the fountain's edge, holding a red umbrella in one hand and a sign that read "ME" in really large letters in the other. When they saw each other, they both busted out in laughter. There was no one else Jennifer would have rather gone to prom with than Scott Webb. Scott looked nervous until she yelled, "Yes," while at the same time having a big huge smile on her face and thinking of how cute the whole thing was.

OR

Text: "Wanna go 2 prom?"

Answer: "K"

Which of these sounds more fun? Right . . . NOT the second one. Even though the second one was advertised in a cell phone commercial, it really cheapens an opportunity to do something in a fun, cute, and romantic way. Now, prom doesn't HAVE to be some big, romantic, spectacular event, but don't you want it to be memorable?

A lot of people have cheapened the process of attraction, communication, and personal interaction. I'm going to remind you again: when a guy actually has to put effort into attaining something, he enjoys it and appreciates it more. This includes girls. Although there are guys who may prefer easy over hard, they cannot appreciate it as much. Plus, do you really want a guy this lazy?

To put it another way, think about jewelry. It's kind of like replacing a precious and rare diamond necklace with a fake plastic one. You might be fooled at first glance. In fact, it might look like it has real diamonds and it might even sparkle like it. Other people might think that it's real and it might even look great with an outfit. That's all fine; there's nothing wrong with fake jewelry, unless of course you think it's real. It is not. It looks like it, but it's a cheaper version, a stripped-down fake replica of the real thing. It is an imposter, and even though it looks great from a distance, up close it is not the real thing. The way we interact with one another can be the same way. It can build up, strengthen, attract, and reinforce great relationships, or it can cheapen them. Luckily this outcome is up to you.

Here is a pretty common conversation I have about texting:

Chad: So, Meredith, are you pretty texty with the guy you are talking about then?

Meredith: I mean, yeah, it's kind of the way that we usually talk. I mean, I think it's like the way that he kind of gets a hold of me first and then we just keep texting.

C: So you said you are confused by him. What are you confused about then?

M: Well, he always says he likes me and stuff and that he wants to do stuff together, like the physical stuff. I guess it makes me feel pretty uncomfortable, and then he asks me all the personal questions and asks for, like, pictures of me kind of posing and stuff . . . but he doesn't really act like he likes me when we're around other people.

C: And this is confusing, huh?

M: Yeah, really confusing, I'm like, what the heck, why does he do that? I don't get it. He won't say those things to me in person, but he texts that way.

C: Well, let me ask you this: you said that the way he IMs you or texts with you makes you uncomfortable, whether it's the questions he asks or the pictures and stuff, right?

M: Yeah.

C: Well, do you still do it? Do you still answer the questions and do the stuff that makes you uncomfortable?

M: (hesitation) . . . Yeah, sometimes I do.

C: How's that working out for you? Is it making him like you more?

M: No, it sucks; I don't understand. He is comfortable talking to me about that stuff in a text, but then he'll act different in person after that.

C: How hard is your heart to get access to, Meredith? Are you as hard to get as punching buttons on a keypad? Does that give access to the most personal things that you can possibly have?

M: Yes . . . I mean no.

C: (interrupting) No, Meredith, the answer is yes. Yes, you are being that easy. I'm not trying to hurt your feelings, but you are saying one thing and doing the opposite. Yes, your heart is easily accessible, and, yes, this boy doesn't have to put forth hardly any effort to know you in a way that can take years by people who are doing it correctly.

Do you want to be that easy, Meredith?

M: No.

C: Then don't be. That's up to you, no one else. And the answer is yes . . . you have to change. You have to for yourself, otherwise you might feel like this throughout your life, and that's sad. That's not what is meant for you, my friend, okay?

I can't tell you how many times I have had conversations just like this one. When you are sitting where I am, and you see all of this confusion and mixed signals, you don't get angry; you just feel compassionate and slightly sad. It's a tragedy that a lot of guys and girls are not learning to communicate in a way that makes them like each other more. Yes, to engage in suggestive conversations over the phone or through texting might make you seem more flirty, more risqué, and a little more exciting more quickly. That's why people, especially guys, do it. But that doesn't mean it's good. It just means it is easier. Many teen guys, if given the easier opportunity, will take it. This is why we need teamwork.

It Is Both WHAT You Say and HOW You Are Saying It

If you want to understand guys, start by understanding communication. If you want to understand attraction and how to be attractive, understand communication. If you want to learn how guys are wired, what to say and not to say to keep their attention, and how you can make attraction greater or worse, start to understand communication.

Dating and attraction are not a game, but at the same

time, yes, they most definitely are. Why? In any game there are rules or guidelines. These exist to provide the most natural, positive, and fair outcome for everyone. When you play the game all backward and sideways, it looks dumb and not many people enjoy it. When people do things really backward, without understanding HOW to interact with the opposite sex, things don't work out well. They just don't. These are not arbitrary guidelines, made up by people; guys and girls have been created differently, with some different needs and different ways of communicating and connecting. God made us to compliment one another, and the more we understand the differences, the more we can have healthy relationships with one another.

This chapter isn't just about LOLs or any other cute text phrases, although it often involves them. It's about communication. It's about how we interact with one another. This interaction is important. How you communicate and how others communicate with you already affects you, and it's not going to stop. It will affect the way your high school experience goes, it will affect all of your friendships, it will affect all of the guys you are ever interested in, and it will even affect marriage when that day comes. The reason is because communicating is about talking and understanding. Talking is meant to communicate meaning, intent, likes, and dislikes. Although we talk every day, some of us more than others, it will take us trying to understand each other every day to get it right. The way you communicate with guys is really important. The way guys communicate with you is equally important.

If you don't understand the natural programming of guys, you may think that you have to do a lot in order to get a guy's attention and interest. But guys aren't wired like girls. They want to pursue you, not have you pursue them. What guys value the most is being successful, and this can include many categories in our life: sports, grades, being funny, or being great at a job one day. One of these many categories includes impressing girls. Guys typically are happiest when a girl is responsive to his attempts to impress her and to gain her interest.

The balance for a girl and a guy is to pursue and respond in the right amounts, at the right time, and in the right way. You don't want to make it impossible, but many girls make it too easy. Guys need a challenge, a job, a task, and we need to understand how to do it correctly. It takes both people to understand how this is going to work.

Quality vs. Quantity

Quality time is more important than quantity time. This is a little principle that is important when you are deciding how available to make yourself to other people. If you decide that your time is valuable, then you are less likely to spend it sending out thousands of text messages and more likely to spend time with your friends doing something fun and enjoying each other's company.

Mysterious Girl

One of the best and also the most frustrating things guys will say about girls is that they can't figure them out. But one of the greatest things about you is that we can't figure you out. You are mysterious. Heck, I know a lot of girls who say they have a hard time figuring themselves out, so imagine what it's like for us. It's also one of God's best designs. There is something incredibly important, natural, and healthy about having a little mystery to you. This means you will want to reserve some of those thoughts, hopes, and feelings for later. Too much of a good thing can still be too much. This includes you.

How accessible are you? Think about your answers to the following questions:

- Are the lines of communication to you always open?
- Are you easy to get a hold of?
- Do you answer all the questions guys ask you, even if they don't feel appropriate or they make you uncomfortable?

A mysterious girl is a healthy girl. If diamonds were

common and were lying around on the ground, they wouldn't be as desirable; they would just be rocks. We don't hunt all over the world for common rocks; it's the ones that are less accessible, harder to find, and therefore more valuable that we desire.

Consider becoming a little more like that diamond and stray away from becoming a rock.

Your Billboard

Would you put a picture of you in a bikini top on a billboard off the highway? No. (If you said yes, that's the wrong answer; change it to no.) Do you think it's any different to display personal things about you via MySpace, picture messaging, or e-mail? No, it really isn't. Just because it may not seem as real as a billboard, you can be assured that to the receiver, it is just as powerful. And an equal number of people can see you on the Internet with skimpy clothes on, in fact probably more.

Posting all of your passions, your body, your emotional state, your heartbreak, and anything else that is really personal in a way that someone only has to click a button to have access to all that information is no different than putting all that stuff on a giant billboard in Times Square. Seriously, you might need to reconsider the message you are sending and how you are sending it.

A lot of girls and guys do this because they do not see the millions of odd people who are on the other end looking at these personal things. If you don't want a creepy old dude staring at pictures of you posing in provocative clothes, then don't post them on the World Wide Web. The key words there are *World Wide* . . . not just your friends. Also, once they are out there, they are there for good. They don't go away, and this needs to be something you strongly consider before you click on the word *post*.

The other motive is usually attention. A lot of people confuse two different types of attention. Positive attention and negative attention are not the same things. There is a common characteristic in girls who are regarded in high esteem. I mean girls who are really valuable and know it. They seem to be more concerned with keeping people away from them than they are attracting people to them—not in a cold way, but in a protective way.

Somewhere along the line people have gotten confused with thinking that more and more attention is positive, when in fact it's usually the opposite. People who are more selective with the people they receive attention from tend to attract higher-caliber people. This is infinitely more important than just attracting lots of people. It's kind of like food. Would you rather have tons of food that is bad for you, or a smaller portion of food that is much healthier? Whichever of these appetites you give into, it will affect you.

Lost in Translation

Sixty to ninety.[1] That's the percentage of communication that does NOT come from words. Experts debate over this stuff, but they put it somewhere between those two numbers. You know what that means? Over half of what you say is not expressed in words. It's the other stuff, the little tiny things like a squinting of the eyes, a scrunch of the eyebrow, a slight movement in your lips that means intrigue, or a great big smile to say you are happy.

Fishing . . . I Mean Texting

Guys like to go fishing. Maybe you do too. I'm just speaking for guys because I am one. Unfortunately there just don't seem to be as many opportunities to pack up and head to the lake these days with our busy schedules, homework, sports, video games, and the Internet. Guess what, though? Guys have adapted. They still go fishing. It just usually doesn't involve fish.

Okay, okay, texting isn't evil. I don't mind texting, if I need something quick or directions or things that are insignificant, but it does very little good beyond that. When it comes to guys choosing the easy route, this can include the way they text with you. Whether or not you believe it, it is not easy or natural for guys to say vulnerable things to a girl, to tell her he is interested in her, or to tell her personal things about him.

As too many girls know, they often find themselves having conversations via text that should be done in person. This is not a coincidence, and this is usually not good either. If the guy doesn't like your answer, he can just click *x*, or not write back, or avoid it. Many times it sets up a system that allows them to weigh lots of options (girls) and communicate easily with many of them until they get an answer they want. They may do this without even realizing what they are doing. Guys aren't as sinister as some may think; they just need guidance.

Don't be a piece of lettuce at a buffet bar, one option for the picking. If you want to hear a rule of thumb that is applicable here, then consider this strongly: don't ever let a guy say or ask you something that he can't say to you in person. I say this to guys too, but it's usually you that this applies to more. This is a natural buffer, a safety device, and a barrier that protects you and lets others know that if they want to ask you something important, then they can do it face-to-face with eye contact and real words.

Don't Text My Heart

Maybe that should be a bold T-shirt that every girl wears. Of course it could be cute too and made in different colors to go with your outfits. Don't worry, I've planned ahead. What I actually mean is that it is so incredibly heart-breaking to see girls give people access to their hearts, minds, and feelings over a cheap cell-phone key pad. This is not romantic, this is not healthy, and this does not usually end well. If someone wants to get to know you in any emotional or vulnerable way, it is better that they muster up the courage to do it in person. Here's the kicker: only if YOU DECIDE you feel like hearing it. What I mean is that you don't have to have conversations if you don't want to. You don't have to answer or even look at a text just because someone sends it to you. You also NEVER need to feel uncomfortable about stopping a conversation that is headed down Inappropriate Avenue. You don't have to accept or internalize all the words someone is trying to say to you, and I find that girls who understand their value have a firm authority and confidence in the fact that the decision is up to them.

Here are some other things you might think about when it comes to texting:

- It is really easy to say something you don't mean or something you wouldn't really say in person.
- It can be rude if you are constantly texting when others are around. It makes the people you are hanging out with think you aren't interested in them.
- Texting can be suspicious. Who are you always

texting? This is a factor especially when you're dating someone—it can create insecurity.
- Texting gives people access to your life that you may not want. It's really easy to pop in and out of someone's life in a very noncommittal way.
- It's lacking in context, nonverbal meaning, and tone.

Facebook, MySpace, and these kinds of Web sites all have some significant pitfalls as well:

- Girls and guys often put up pictures that can border on inappropriate and even pornographic.
- Do you really want a person to get to know you on your social networking site?
- All kinds of information are passed around, and many girls let strangers have all kinds of access to their life.
- Even if it's dudes you may "know" but not very well, you both say stuff in a way that requires no commitment, no courage, or hardly anything that takes much effort.

Do You Hear That? Me Neither

Silence is golden. And sometimes it's what you don't say that affects guys. Being mysterious and not giving everything away is really important in the communication process. Your words are valuable, so don't waste them. You don't need to feel obligated to answer every question that is asked to you. I don't and I'm a guy. In fact, I find that this is very valuable. There is an old adage that says, "When you listen you have all the power, and when you talk you give it away." While I'm not telling you to stop talking, you might consider that it's empowering to not feel pressured to respond to every question or engage in every conversation. This is part of setting boundaries and saying no, and sometimes your silence can get a message across just as strongly as words could.

Make sure your story is told to others in words, in person, and not in text. You won't be as confused, and you'll save on your monthly text bill.

How Mysterious Are You?

1. You have joined Facebook or another social networking site, and you are about to put some pictures up. Your aim will mostly be:
   a. to impress your guy "friends" with how physically attractive you are
   b. to impress your girl and guy friends with your looks and your lifestyle

c. to share snapshots of exciting events in your life with friends

2. You're chatting to your mom in the kitchen when your boyfriend texts you. What do you do?
   a. text back immediately
   b. ask your mom if she minds if you quickly text your boyfriend back
   c. reply when you've finished chatting to your mom

3. To get a guy's attention, you should be responsive to any attempt he makes to impress you and gain your attention.
   a. true
   b. false
   c. sometimes true

Add up your score:

A = 3 B = 2 C = 1

Your results:

8–9

» You are not very mysterious. You try too hard to impress guys and keep them happy with you, leaving very little room for mystery.

5–7

» You try hard to be mysterious, but are not quite getting it right. You try to play hard to get, but can't resist trying to impress others. You send out conflicting signals.

3–4

» Well done! You are mysterious in the right way.

Chapter 12

can speak clearly

Living on Buses

I spent most of the summer on a bus. It was orange, huge, and had a nice diesel smell to it. I didn't sneak onto this bus or steal it, because I don't steal buses. I was doing a summer tour to promote a book and a conference for teens. They wanted me to go around on this giant orange tour bus all over the country and talk to teens. This was pretty much my dream job. When else would I be able to travel all over the country, spend most of the summer outside, hang out in truck stops in the middle of the night, shower from a hanging shower bag in a field, see both oceans and everything in between, and, of course, get to spend two and a half months talking to kids from all around the country?

If there was a youth-group event or meeting, and it was when we were coming through town, our bus would pull in for the evening, we would hang out with the kids, I would talk for a while, and sometimes people would even feed us. Pretty cool. I ate more cookies than I should have, but what am I gonna do . . . be Captain Rude Pants and turn down someone's homemade hospitality cookie?

Answer . . . NO, I am not rude. I ate every cookie, and I did it because of the compassion in my heart.

Anyway, when I was talking with the youth-group girls, I would ask them a simple question, and I asked it in a very relaxed and nonthreatening way. They all had their eyes closed, so I don't think there was a reason to lie about this one. I simply asked them to point their little finger up if they felt okay with saying or feeling the following: "I am really valuable." I wanted to know how many girls felt pretty comfortable or confident saying to themselves that they are really special, they have value, and they don't feel awkward or wrong or weird about feeling that way. How many girls in a group do you think would raise their hands? What number would you guess on average of a group of say one hundred girls?

Do you know how many girls actually said they felt valuable and felt comfortable feeling that way? The answer is two. Two of them. It wasn't two girls in each group. It was two girls the entire summer!!!!!!! TWO, one, two, 2 out of everyone I met!

I was overwhelmed and confused. I know that everyone can occasionally want to change things about themselves, improve who they are, the way they look, yadda yadda . . . but do people really not feel valuable at all? I am absolutely astounded by how many teens, girls in particular, aren't even at the place where they can confidently declare that "I am valuable" and feel comfortable saying that.

How Much Do You Value Yourself?

1. How comfortable are you with saying, "I am really valuable"?
   a. Very *uncomfortable*—it makes you think of a certain cosmetics advertising campaign, and you do not feel "worth it" like *those* gorgeous girls
   b. you know you should, but you don't feel right thinking or saying it
   c. totally!

2. Who would you most like to be?
   - **a.** your favorite female celebrity
   - **b.** a slightly better-looking and more successful you, with a more polished personality
   - **c.** you're honestly happy being you

3. Where do you most look for affirmation?
   - **a.** in how much people (including guys) pay attention to you
   - **b.** in your achievements
   - **c.** in thanking God each day for making you *you*

Add up your score:

A = 3 B = 2 C = 1

Your results:

8–9

» Very little. Unfortunately, you try to determine your value according to the unrealistic expectations of the world around you.

5–7

» A little. You don't put much value in yourself now, but have the idealistic hope that you can increase your value in the future.

3–4

» A lot! You understand what your true value is, and look for it in the correct place.

Baby Steps

First things first, right? You put one foot in front of the other to learn how to walk. Why would it be different when it comes to our relationships? How are we supposed to understand most things in life if we can't accept that we are valuable? Do you think other people are valuable? Yes, probably, most likely, you can look at someone and say that they are valuable . . . I mean why wouldn't they be? It's not hard to realize that people in general have value. So why does a person have a hard time realizing that he or she is an individual of value?

He Likes Her

I was talking to a younger buddy of mine. He likes this girl a lot. He is way into her, has been friends with her for a long time, and is at a place where he really is ready to date. He likes her enough that he is taking the steps to start a strong and lasting relationship with her. And she digs him too. She, in fact, likes him equally as much as he likes her. It's really cool to watch.

There is just one stumbling block. She has something in the way of their relationship. That thing is her opinion about herself. Overall she seems like a really great girl. She is very smart, very funny, very creative . . . but she has a problem. A problem that a lot of girls have . . . a dad hasn't reassured her of her value. And guess what? It starts to get in the way of a lot of stuff. She might try to look to her boyfriend for more affirmation than he is able to give her. She might start to get really insecure that there is something wrong with her, she's not good enough, maybe there's a better girl, or maybe he isn't thinking about her as much as she is him, and the list will always go on.

I was talking with my buddy about this when it simply occurred to us: man, a lot of this stuff would simply work itself out if she was more comfortable with herself. It would be a lot healthier if she really liked herself. And I know that sounds really simple, maybe too simple, but it's still true. So let's flip it around and think about this a different way.

Baggage Boys

What if a guy you knew was constantly thinking he wasn't good enough, had low self-esteem, didn't like himself, and was always comparing himself to other guys? And while some do this, guys don't tend to do this as often as girls. If you are thinking about dating a guy, don't you want to know that he is comfortable with who he is? That he feels comfortable in his own skin and he isn't always trying to be something or someone else? Interestingly, a lot of girls say the opposite, that guys like themselves too much. You should know that this isn't usually true. A lot of us have the same struggles you do; we're just better at hiding it. Guys also need to learn to be comfortable with the skin, the body, the face, the mind, and the heart that God gave them. If we need to do this in order to be healthy, the same goes for you.

There is nothing more right, more natural and healthy, more attractive (in every sense of the word) than a girl who genuinely likes who she is. It outweighs her looks, her outfits, her car, her hair, and all of the other things that a girl puts so much effort into. And those things will never replace the simple fact that learning to like yourself and appreciate yourself is the most important and attractive thing you can ever do.

This book is about relationships, but more importantly, it's about the relationship you have with yourself. Maybe you take the time to evaluate the relationship you have with yourself, but in case you don't, perhaps now would be a good time to start.

- Are you honest and evaluative about how you treat yourself?

- Are you your own best friend or your own worst enemy?

- Can you name five traits that are great about you off the top of your head?

- Are you confident in front of both your friends and your family?

- Do you speak to yourself in a kind way or do you tend to get down on yourself?

- Do you like the way you look or do you spend most of the time thinking about ways you can change something about you?

- Would you tolerate someone else treating you the way you treat yourself?

Real Love

When it all boils down to one thing, it often boils down to love. Really, that's what you have been reading about; why it's important to value yourself, and how to value other people, including boys. That's what love is. A lot of people don't really take time to understand what love means and it ends up biting them later. One really important thing to figure out is the difference between real love and something that looks a lot like love. It is called infatuation, and although it looks similar, it is different.

I am sure you want a guy who understands what it means to care. Likewise, guys like girls who understand how to care. Here are some things to think about when it comes to the idea of love and infatuation. I hope you will consider them not only when it comes to you, but as it applies to all the people in your life now and in the future.

1. Infatuation almost always leaps quickly into bloom. Love usually takes root more slowly and it grows with time.

2. Infatuation is accompanied by a sense of uncertainty. You are stimulated, thrilled, and filled with a kind of feverish excitement. You are miserable when he or she is absent. You can't wait until you see them again. Love brings a feeling of security. You are warm with a sense of nearness even when he or she is far away. Miles do not really separate you. You want the person near, but you know you can wait.

3. When you are infatuated, you may lose your appetite. You may daydream a lot. You can't concentrate. You can't study. You can't keep your mind on your work. You may be short-tempered and unpleasant with your family. When you're in love, you're just the opposite. You can be sensible about your loved one. You feel more secure and trusting. Love gives you new energy and inspires you to do more than you ever dreamed possible.

4. Infatuation brings that feeling that you can't wait. You can't take the chance of losing him or her. When you're in love, you know you can wait. You are sure of one another. You can plan for your future with complete confidence.

5. Infatuation may stem from a desire for self gratification. You wish to be identified with the person. You want your friends to see that he or she has chosen you. When in love, there is always a deep concern for the welfare of the loved one; you are far more focused on him or her then you are on yourself.

6. Infatuation may be merely physical attraction. If you are honest, you may discover that it is often difficult to enjoy each other unless you are leading up to sexual activity. Sex is also a natural and spontaneous part of love, but only a part. If your love is real, you will enjoy a deep friendship with a loved one. You will truly enjoy each other without being physical.

7. Infatuated couples may find it easy to disagree. When you're in love, although your personalities may be quite different, there is an eagerness to hear the other side; to give as well as to take; to compromise.

8. Infatuation hardly ever thinks of the far future. What will the person be like thirty years from now? What kind of parent will he or she make? What kind of home life will we have? Love is much more concerned with the future, wanting to grow and build a life together.

9. You may fall into infatuation, but you never "fall" in love.

10. Infatuation may lead you to do things you feel are wrong, things that worry you. But love will never pressure you to compromise your values or violate your boundaries.

11. Infatuation may lead you to try to become someone you are not to try to win the person's approval or acceptance. Love embraces your differences, celebrating who you are as a unique and valuable human being. Love brings out the best in both people. "Why do I love you? I love you not only for what you are, but for what I am when I am with you."[1]

Finally, a Real Answer

I decided to save the simplest and the most important thing for last. I hope I didn't bore you on the way here. The important thing is that you are here, and now I have something I would really like you to know.

You are valuable. Sounds simple, right? Try saying that out loud to yourself while you are alone and see how comfortable you feel. Try picturing saying that to a guy if he is pestering you, or pressuring you, or making you feel uncomfortable, or discouraging you. How many of you could comfortably say, "Hey, stop making me feel bad. I like myself and I'm comfortable in my own skin, so leave me alone?"

And the point of this book is to share with you six words . . .

GUYS LIKE GIRLS WHO LIKE THEMSELVES.

Picture a guy who is always saying he's ugly. What if he constantly is talking about how other guys have great hair and are more muscular than he is? What if this guy is constantly concerned that you aren't going to like him, so he gets insecure, crowds you, avoids you, or always says he thinks you don't like him? What if he gets down on himself when someone says something bad about him, and he is always wondering if people are gossiping about him? What if he chooses his friends not just because he actually likes them but because he feels the need to fit in somewhere doing something all the time? What if, when you really take a look at him, he doesn't seem to like himself much at all?

Would you want to date this guy? Would you want to start a relationship with someone who thinks of himself this way? Does this sound like someone whom you could really enjoy or someone whose personal identity is going to get in the way of your relationship? It's an easy answer. They might be nice, good-looking, smart, musical, athletic, or funny. However, there's one really important thing. If they don't at the very least LIKE themselves, it will be hard to have a good relationship with them.

Now here is a question for you. Do you think guys are any different from you?

Honestly, do you really think that a guy wants to be with, around, or dating a girl who isn't comfortable with who she is? No. Healthy guys don't want that. There is nothing wrong with liking yourself. In fact, it's wrong to not like yourself. It means you are being irrational, and it means you aren't looking at yourself the way God looks at you. Guys need you to like yourself. And if you are struggling with your self-image, you won't just suddenly like yourself one day. It doesn't magically happen. It means you have to start right now. It means that unless you start getting really comfortable in your own skin, you are going to feel itchy forever.

Guys like girls who like themselves. This is just the beginning. In order to do anything else in the best way, you have to like who you are. You have to at least say to yourself and believe it, "I mean, yeah, I do like who I am." Unless you do this, we can never really see you the way that God sees you, which by the way . . . is beautiful.

It sounds simple, but this point flows deep down into our hearts and our souls. Notice I didn't say girls who act confident, act all sassy, are conceited, or are really into themselves. I said guys like a girl who likes herself. And it's not until you can really accept the fact that you have value that other people can love that about you too.

I wish you all the best in this journey of yours. Thanks for not laughing at me when I shared these thoughts, although I guess I wouldn't know if you did. Enjoy the journey, and learn along the way. You won't be perfect, but who wants that anyway? It's boring. Instead of perfection, I hope you will learn to value yourself more every day. You need to do that and guys need you to do that.

You are someone's future. You are already of more value to someone than you could understand.

We probably haven't met, but if we do, I would like you. I hope that you can too.

Chapter 13

can read directions

There might be a lot of information to digest in this book. I wanted to make sure I left you with some concrete suggestions on real-life relationships and dating scenarios. I also wanted to thank the thousands of teens who write and share their opinions and ask a lot of questions. It is an honor to share my thoughts with you, and as long as you will allow me to, I will continue to talk and write to you.

When I talk about the issue of dating, I get asked a lot of

similar questions about the subject. While it's nearly impossible to address them all, I have been able to categorize them and offer some suggestions for you to put in your pocket and take with you . . . kind of like "directions" for your dating map. It's pretty simple, and I hope it will help. There are things you should DO and NOT DO in the dating process. I hope you will take them into consideration. You deserve to have great teenage years. You deserve to have fun and enjoy your relationships. You can do this, and I hope and pray that you will. So here are some general dos and don'ts for the world of dating.

Chad's Don't-Do-While-Dating List

Here are a few other things I have learned—or smarter people have shared—about what *not* to do while dating:

1. Don't date someone you wouldn't be friends with. When you're relaxed you'll be more of the natural you, which is really important when you start to date someone. If dating is a continuation of friendship, there is no way to date someone whom you wouldn't consider a friend.

2. Don't date for attention. Lots of people fall into this trap. It means you are not mature enough to know the healthy reason that you would want to start dating—that you genuinely like that person and want to get to know

them more. Dating to get the attention you feel you need is not the same thing. It also usually means that there are some big insecurity hurdles to overcome before you can date in a healthy way. A guy will never be able to give you all of the attention you feel you need. And here's a secret: we don't want to. We want to enjoy you for the right reasons.

3. Don't date because you are lonely. This might make you feel good for a while, but it will not cure your loneliness. You would be much better off getting involved in other things, like activities at school, a club, sports, or anything that fills your time in a constructive way. It's not fair to you or anyone else to date to make up for a lack of something.

4. Don't just think about dating right here, right now. Remember to look ahead. It is a process to get to know the opposite sex; think about it in that light. You would be better off realizing you will probably date more than one person and viewing dating as a way to learn about someone. Dating is also where you learn what you do and don't like, and what you do and do not tolerate.

5. Don't try to date-rescue people. Don't ever date someone expecting to change them, especially when it comes to the faith thing. That is not your job; it's God's. God works in the hearts of people in his own time. If someone is struggling or you see some way that they need help, you are better off being friends with them than trying to start a romantic relationship.

If you are standing on a chair and you want to help someone else up onto that chair, beware. It's much easier for them to accidentally pull you off of that chair than for you to help them onto it. People who aren't living healthy lives are more likely to pull you down than you are to lift them up. Be their friend, not their girlfriend.

In the fairy tale, the princess kisses a frog and it turns into a prince, but it's just that—a fairy tale. It doesn't happen like that in real life, and you probably shouldn't spend your time kissing frogs anyway, that's just gross.

6. Don't try and adapt to what you think someone else will like. You will regret it and you will end up feeling worse. Not everyone will like you and you can't make them. You were created to be you and no one else. The people who are supposed to be in your life will be in it because you are being yourself instead of adapting to what you think others prefer.

7. Don't date people who don't respect you or other people. Bad things happen when people do this. Girls find themselves disrespected, verbally abused, sexually abused, and other terrible things. If someone doesn't show respect as a personality trait, then don't waste your time and compromise your self-respect by putting yourself in that environment. Here is a simple rule: if they don't respect others, they won't respect you either.

8. Be careful with the opposite magnet. You may feel like someone who is your opposite is your missing puzzle piece,

that together you make the perfect person. If you feel shy and timid, you might be attracted to a guy who seems strong and confident. This person just seems to make up for everything you are not. The problem with this is that it can stunt your own growth. God wants us to depend on him first, not on the skills and gifts of others. Don't fall for someone who is outgoing because you are shy. You want to be interested in someone for how they encourage you to grow, love, and move toward God. You do NOT want to fall for someone because they are what you are not.[1]

Chad's Dating List of Dos

1. Going to a public place is a good idea, especially if you don't know the dude very well. However, going to the movies is dumb. Seriously. Sorry if that offends you. I don't hate movies. I like them very much, especially the ones where stuff blows up. But if dating is about getting to know each other, do something that will allow you to TALK.

2. Think about what makes guys comfortable too. The reason why putt-putting, for example, is a good idea is because it gives room for both people to talk and it keeps guys comfortable. Sitting and staring at each other for hours at a dinner table is NOT comfortable.

3. Don't be afraid to suggest what to do on a date; sometimes we aren't very creative. But once you give us an idea,

we can really make it fun and "romantic," if you're into that sort of thing.

4. Learn to say NO. Being able to tell others no will help to keep you out of situations that can jeopardize your well-being. It's really easy to spell too.

5. Pop in your favorite "chick flick" and watch it carefully. See how the main characters interact and how different it may be from real life. Take note when they go on dates. What do they do? What makes it comfortable or uncomfortable? Is it realistic?

6. GO ON GROUP DATES/HANGOUTS! These are great because there is little pressure and discomfort. Plus, having a few extra sets of eyes on the guy you like can help with valuable friendship-insight.

7. Create and set your boundaries ahead of time, so that in the moment you won't have to decide what you are and are not comfortable with. Having boundaries means you will need to express your needs when someone has crossed yours. This can be difficult sometimes, but it is part of being a healthy person. Boundaries are not meant to be pushed. They are there to help keep us and others from crossing lines that we have decided should not be crossed. Boundaries are there to protect you and to help you have the best relationships possible. This will attract the right people to your life, and equally important, it will keep away from your life the people who won't be good for you.

8. Do make sure that friendship is first. Even if you have strong feelings for someone, it is incredibly important to learn how to be their friend. If the relationship grows, so will your friendship. If it does not, you will be more likely to still have a friend. Friendship is the most important ingredient in any successful relationship.

9. Do remember that God likes you. He doesn't want you to be taller; he likes you the way you are. He created you. He has a plan for you. He has someone special for your life. So do remember to put your trust and faith in him. It is where your true image will be found, and I promise, it is a fantastic image.

10. Do remember this: GUYS LIKE GIRLS WHO LIKE THEMSELVES. Liking yourself is the beginning. You can't move forward in healthy relationships with anyone until you start to understand that you are valuable and to be comfortable with this.

11. Have fun!

Acknowledgments

extra-special high fives

Okay, I didn't want to make you read this because you probably won't know who in the world I'm talking about. There are some pretty influential people in my life who helped with the contribution to this book. Not with the words—yes, I write all my own books, thank you very much—but with the shaping of the way I think, my experiences, my friendships, and a lot of laughter. You give me a very large pallet of colors to paint a picture with.

Amy and Mary: Thanks for taking a chance on me. You are two of the most respectable women I have known.

D Jones, Sean with 4 first names, Loogie, Ryan, Jimmers, D Mort, Talbs, Benny B, J Mo, Nutty, Fay Bumper, BW Coate, M. Joyce, Reesy, Hawk boys, Nat's whole band, and many other great guys in my life. Thanks for having all of those nicknames, for being there when I have needed you, and for unintentionally being a great group of guys. Also thanks for the incredible, and slightly odd, amount of guy-time that you all provide. You are very rare, like delicate roses. I'm kidding, mostly. You guys are great, and thanks for being so influential, even if you didn't mean to be.

To Carole and Healthy Visions: You are incredibly caring, passionate, and empowering. You pretty much forced me to believe I have a lot to offer, which is kind of dangerous, but now I am ever so thankful for that.

My colleagues and friends at Revolve and Thomas Nelson: I'm very upset that you are all so great. That means that things only go down from here. I could not ask for a better, more trustworthy, hard-working group of people. It is an honor to know and work with all of you.

notes

Introduction

1. *The Art of Loving Well: A Character Education Curriculum for Today's Teenagers* (Boston: Boston University, 1998), 92.
2. Ibid., 91.

Chapter 3

1. *Newsletter of the Gallup Youth Survey* 8, no. 10 (June 2001).

Chapter 4

1. Bill and Pam Farrel, *Men Are Like Waffles—Women Are Like Spaghetti* (Eugene, OR: Harvest House, 2001).

2. Centers for Disease Control and Prevention, National Center for Health Statistics, Division of Vital Statistics, various years, http://www.cdc.gov/.
3. Lillian Glass, PhD, *He Says, She Says* (New York: Pedigree, 1993).
4. Chad Eastham, *The Truth About Guys* (Nashville: Thomas Nelson, 2006).

Chapter 5

1. Carol Emery Normandi and Laurelee Roark, *Over It: A Teen's Guide to Getting Beyond Obsessions with Food and Weight* (Novato, CA: New World Library, 2001).
2. Benjamin R. Barber, *Consumed: How Markets Corrupt Children, Infantilize Adults, and Swallow Citizens Whole* (New York: W.W. Norton & Company Inc, 2007).
3. 1 Corinthians 13:4–7 (NIV).
4. *The Heritage Foundation: A Book of Charts*, http://www.heritage.org.
5. Bernice Kranner, "Are You a Normal Guy?" *American Demographics* 21, no. 3 (March 1999): 19.
6. The President's Council on Physical Fitness and Sports, http://www.fitness.gov.
7. Margo Maine, PhD, and Joe Kelly, *The Body Myth: Women and the Pressure to Be Perfect* (Hoboken, NJ: Wiley & Sons, 2005).
8. Department of Psychiatry at the University of Minnesota, http://www.med.umn.edu/psychiatry/research/eating/home.html.

Chapter 6

1. *Newsletter of the Gallup Youth Survey* 8, no. 10 (June 2001).
2. Diana Romeo, "Real Life Mean Girls," *Justine*, October–November 2007.

Chapter 8

1. *GL Magazine*, October 2007, 66–83; Josh McDowell's personal notes on Teen Statistics.

Chapter 9

1. Centers for Disease Control and Prevention, National Center for Health Statistics, Division of Vital Statistics, various years, http://www.cdc.gov/; D. G. Curtis, "Perspectives on Acquaintance Rape," The American Academy of Experts in Traumatic Stress, http://www.aaets.org/arts/art13.htm/.
2. Dr. Henry Cloud and Dr. John Townsend, *Boundaries in Dating* (Grand Rapids: Zondervan Publishing, 2000), 27.
3. Ibid., 29.

Chapter 11

1. Michael Argyle, *Bodily Communication*, 2nd ed. (Madison: International Universities Press, 1988); Judith L. Hanna, *To Dance Is Human: A Theory of Nonverbal Communication* (Chicago: University of Chicago Press, 1987); Mark L. Knapp and Judith A. Hall, *Nonverbal Communication in Human Interaction*, 5th ed. (Wadsworth: Thomas Learning, 2007); J. K. Burgoon, D. B. Buller, and W. G. Woodall, *Nonverbal Communication: The Unspoken Dialogue*, 2nd ed. (New York: McGraw-Hill, 1996); D. B. Givens, "Body Speak: What Are You Saying?" *Successful Meetings*, October 2000, 51.

Chapter 12

1. From the poem "Why Do I Love You?" by Carolyn Davies, in *The Art of Loving Well: A Character Education Curriculum for Today's Teenagers* (Boston University: Boston, 1998), 153–54.

Chapter 13

1. Dr. Henry Cloud and Dr. John Townsend, *Boundaries in Dating* (Grand Rapids: Zondervan, 2000), 145–46.